Getting Started with the Market Research Application

SAS Institute Inc.
SAS Campus Drive
Cary, NC 27513

The correct bibliographic citation for this manual is as follows: SAS Institute Inc., *Getting Started with the Market Research Application*, Cary, NC: SAS Institute Inc., 1997. 56 pp.

Getting Started with the Market Research Application

ISBN 1-58025-059-9

SAS Institute Inc., SAS Campus Drive, Cary, North Carolina 27513.

1st printing, October 1997

Credits

Documentation

Writing	William Duckworth, Robert E. Derr
Editing	Donna M. Sawyer, Maura Stokes
Editorial Support	Patsy J. Poole
Production Support and Cover Design	Creative Solutions Division
Review	Gerardo I. Hurtado, Warren F. Kuhfeld, Mike Stockstill, Maura Stokes

Software

Development	Wayne E. Watson, Warren R. Kuhfeld
Testing	Gregory D. Goodwin

Support Groups

Quality Assurance	Robert P. Agnelli, Katherine M. DeRusso, Frank Lassiter, Gerardo I. Hurtado, Jack Weiss

Getting Started with the Market Research Application

Table of Contents

Getting Started with the Market Research Application

Market research focuses on assessing the preferences and choices of consumers and potential consumers. The Market Research Application (MRA) of SAS/STAT software is an intuitive point-and-click interface that provides statistical and graphical techniques for market research data analysis. The application provides statistical methods such as conjoint analysis, correspondence analysis, discrete choice analysis, multidimensional scaling, and multidimensional preference analysis. This documentation illustrates the use of the Market Research Application by providing a step-by-step discussion of examples* for each of the market research techniques. It does not describe the market research methodologies; however, numerous references are provided to other documentation that discusses these methods.

Overview

Investigators in the field of market research are interested in how consumers make decisions when they choose to buy products. What attributes are important? Do all people make decisions in the same way? If not, how do they differ? What are the perceptual schemes that people use in their purchasing decisions?

The Market Research Application provides easy access to five important types of data analyses commonly used in market research. These five types of analyses are

- conjoint analysis
- correspondence analysis
- discrete choice analysis
- multidimensional scaling
- multidimensional preference analysis

The analyses described in this documentation can be used with many different types of data. The Market Research Application makes these analyses easy to perform.

What Is Conjoint Analysis?

Conjoint analysis is used to evaluate consumers' stated preferences. If products are composed of attributes, conjoint analysis determines which combinations of attribute levels are most preferred by consumers. Consumers indicate their preferences by rating (or ranking) a number of hypothetical products. Conjoint analysis assumes

*To update the examples provided with the software in Release 6.12, please see the section "Updating Samples for Release 6.12" on page 54.

that consumers make purchases by trading off product attributes. The ability to analyze several attributes at once distinguishes conjoint analysis from market research methods where each attribute is studied separately. Conjoint analysis helps you discover how consumers make trade-offs among the available attribute combinations. Usually, conjoint analysis consists of main-effects analyses of variance with ordinally-scaled dependent variables. Consumer preferences are the dependent variables, and product attributes are the independent variables. The following are some of the questions that can be answered by performing a conjoint analysis:

- How important is each product attribute to consumers?
- Which existing products do consumers prefer?
- What combination of product attributes do consumers prefer most?
- How well will my product do in the current market?

What Is Correspondence Analysis?

Correspondence analysis characterizes the associations between the levels of two or more categorical variables by performing a weighted principal component analysis of a contingency table. The results of a correspondence analysis include a graphical representation of the association between the rows and columns of the table. The plot contains points for each row and each column of the table. Rows with similar patterns of counts produce points that are close together, and columns with similar patterns of counts produce points that are close together. Simple correspondence analysis analyzes a contingency table made up of one or more column variables and one or more row variables. Multiple correspondence analysis analyzes the relationships among a set of categorical variables. The following are some of the questions that can be answered by performing a correspondence analysis:

- Who are my customers?
- Who else should be my customers?
- What new products should I create?
- Who should I target with my new products?

What Is Discrete Choice Analysis?

Discrete choice analysis is used to evaluate consumer choice. In discrete choice analysis, each consumer chooses products from sets of products. A set of products is called a *choice set*. Each consumer may be asked to choose from each of several different choice sets. The attributes of the product that define the choices are called *choice attributes* to distinguish them from other attributes that may be of interest but do not contribute to the definition of the choices. For example, you may want to include in the analysis demographic variables that are related to the consumers. The following are some of the questions that can be answered by performing a discrete choice analysis.

- What attributes contribute to the choices made by consumers?
- Which combination of attribute levels is most likely to be chosen by consumers?
- What is the expected market share of my product?

What Is Multidimensional Scaling?

Multidimensional scaling (MDS) uses consumer judgments of product similarities (or differences) to produce a map of the perceived relationships among the products. The following are some of the questions that can be answered by performing multidimensional scaling:

- Which products do consumers see as similar to my product?
- What attributes do consumers use to assess similarity among products?

What Is Multidimensional Preference Analysis?

Multidimensional preference (MDPREF) *analysis* is used to analyze product preference data. In MDPREF analysis, consumers are asked to rate products (typically existing products). Unlike conjoint and discrete choice analysis, MDPREF analysis does not display product attributes. MDPREF analysis is a principal component analysis of a data matrix with columns that correspond to consumers and with rows that correspond to products. The analysis results in a plot that reveals patterns of consumer preference for the products. The following are some of the questions that can be answered by performing a multidimensional preference analysis:

- Who are my customers?
- Who else should be my customers?
- What new products should I create?
- Who should I target with my new products?
- Which products are preferred?
- What product attributes determine preference?
- How are products perceived?

Table 1. Summary of MRA Analyses and their Objectives

Analysis	Objective
conjoint analysis	to evaluate consumer preferences for various combinations of product attributes by having respondents rate or rank their preferred choices
correspondence analysis	to study the associations between the levels of two or more categorical variables to characterize current consumers and determine target consumers
discrete choice analysis	to determine the likelihood of consumers choosing products with given attributes by having respondents select products from each of several choice sets
multidimensional scaling	to determine which products are perceived by consumers as being similar or different and construct a perceptual map.
multidimensional preference analysis	to use consumer preferences to simultaneously map consumers and products. The product attributes are not stated by the researcher.

How to Perform Analyses

Each analysis available in the Market Research Application follows the same basic steps:

1. Select a data set and an analysis.
2. Define the roles of the variables in the analysis.
3. View a plot that summarizes the analysis.
4. View the other results of the analysis.

You invoke the application by issuing the command **`market`** on any command line. The first window that displays requires you to select a data set and an analysis. This initial window is the starting point for all new analyses, and it displays the following:

- libraries available to the application
- data sets contained in the available libraries
- the last analysis performed on each data set
- a drop-down list for selecting an analysis
- a pop-up menu for viewing the data and its attributes
- a pop-up menu for working with the sample data sets

To create sample* data sets, click the Samples button and select Create Sample Data Sets from the pop-up menu; the data sets that you create are placed in the SASUSER directory. These sample data sets are used throughout this documentation. In the following window, the sample SAS data set TIRES is selected from the library SASUSER.

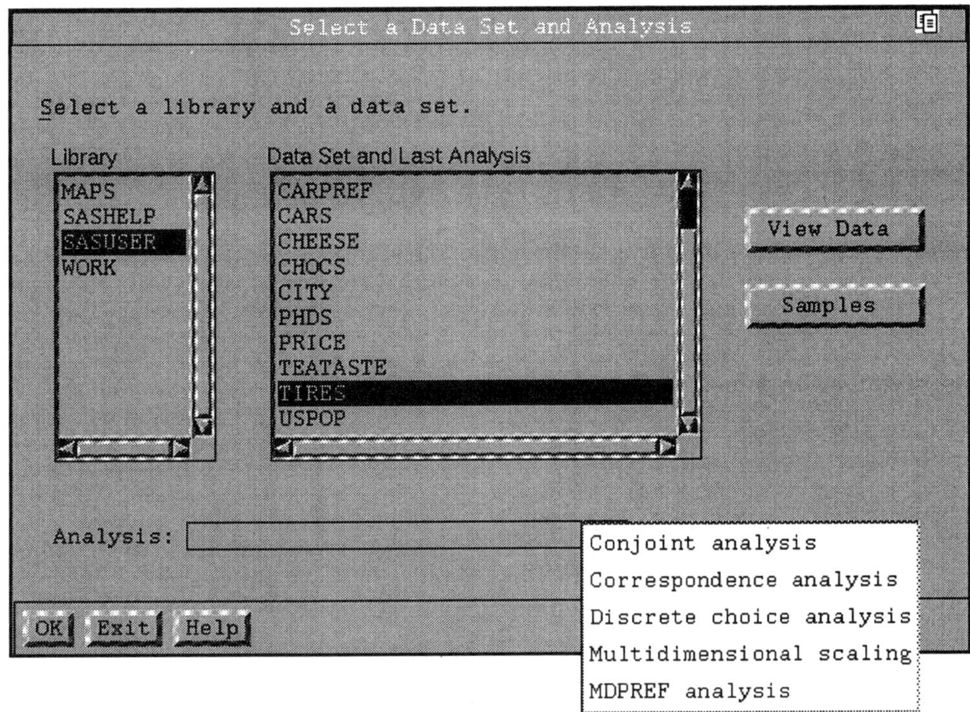

Figure 1. Select a Data Set and Analysis

You can select the library and data set by clicking on the desired names in the Library and Data Set and Last Analysis list boxes. To select an analysis, click the down arrow button to the right of the Analysis list box and then click on the desired analysis name.

You can view either the data values or the variable attributes of the selected data set by clicking the View Data button.

After you have selected a data set and an analysis, click the OK button at the bottom left of the window to proceed with the analysis. The Exit button quits the application, and the Help button provides information about various aspects of this window.

*To update the examples provided with the software in Release 6.12, please see the section "Updating Samples for Release 6.12" on page 54.

Conjoint Analysis

This example of conjoint analysis uses data from the TIRES data set. The following four attributes are related to purchasing automobile tires.

Attribute	Values
brand name	TireMax, GoodTreads, RollsAhead
expected tread mileage	40,000, 60,000, 80,000
purchase price	\$45.00, \$60.00, \$75.00
installation cost	\$0.00, \$7.50

Seven consumers are asked to rank in order of preference 18 out of the possible 54 combinations of attribute levels. The 18 combinations are an orthogonal array design. Although rankings are used in this example, preference ratings are frequently used in conjoint analysis. When consumers provide *ratings*, the most preferred products have large ratings; however, when consumers provide *rankings*, the most preferred products have small ranks. The goal of the analysis is to determine the importance of each attribute to the stated preferences of consumers for a potential tire purchase.

Selecting the Input Data Set

Conjoint analysis requires preference and attribute variables. Each row of the data set corresponds to one of the products being evaluated. Each column corresponds to either an attribute of the products or a preference score for the products. In this example, the preference variables are the ranks from the seven respondents, and the attribute variables are the four factors. The following DATA step creates the data set TIRES:

```
data tires;
   input brand $ charges price mileage judge1-judge7;
   datalines;
TireMax     7.50 45.00 40000 17 17  7 14 13 15 14
TireMax     0.00 75.00 40000 18 15 17 17 17 18 17
TireMax     0.00 60.00 60000 15 10  9  9  9  8  1
TireMax     7.50 75.00 60000 16 11 15 12 14 16  6
TireMax     0.00 45.00 80000 13  3  1  1  2  3  9
TireMax     7.50 60.00 80000 14  4  8  4  5  9  8
GoodTreads 0.00 60.00 40000 11 12 13 15 16 12 15
GoodTreads 7.50 75.00 40000 12 14 18 18 18 17 18
GoodTreads 0.00 45.00 60000  9  5  4  7  4  4  3
GoodTreads 7.50 60.00 60000 10  7 10 10 11  6  2
GoodTreads 7.50 45.00 80000  7  2  2  2  3  2 10
GoodTreads 0.00 75.00 80000  8  6 12  5  6  7 11
RollsAhead 0.00 45.00 40000  5 16  6 13 12 14 13
RollsAhead 7.50 60.00 40000  6 13 11 16 15 13 16
RollsAhead 7.50 45.00 60000  3  8  5  8  7  5  4
RollsAhead 0.00 75.00 60000  4  9 14 11 10 11  5
RollsAhead 0.00 60.00 80000  1  1  3  3  1  1  7
RollsAhead 7.50 75.00 80000  2 18 16  6  8 10 12
;
```

From the **Analysis** list box (shown in Figure 1), select Conjoint analysis and click the OK button to proceed with the analysis.*

Defining the Variables

From the Conjoint Analysis Variable Selection window, you can assign variable roles and set other options that are related to the conjoint analysis.

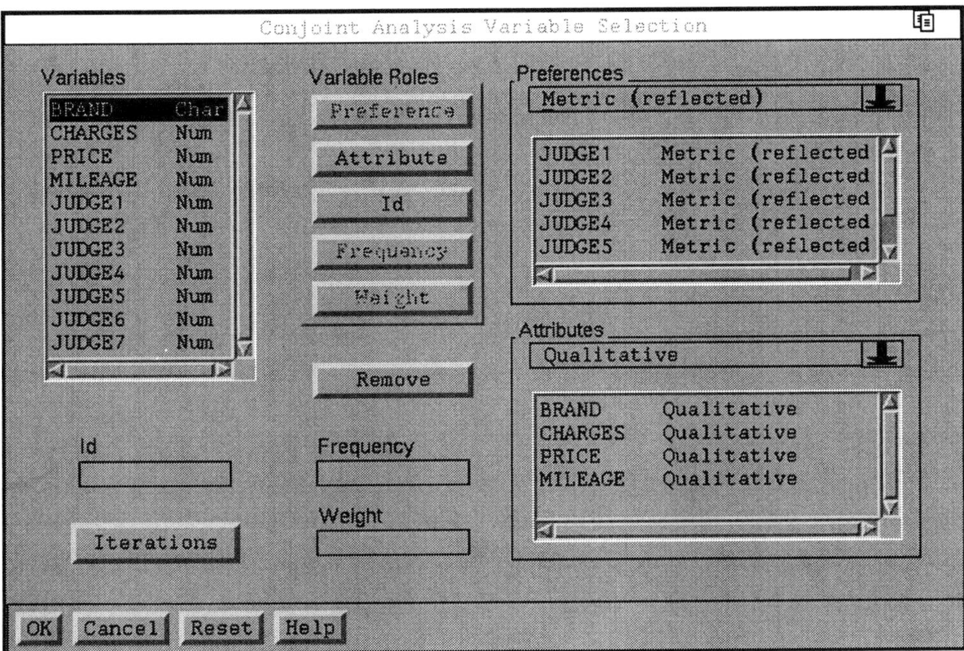

Figure 2. Conjoint Analysis Variable Selection

All variables in the data set TIRES are listed in the **Variables** list box; you can select a variable by clicking on its name. The variable type is also listed to the right of each variable name. For example, BRAND is a character variable (Char), and CHARGES is a numeric variable (Num).

Preference and attribute variables must be defined for a conjoint analysis. You must also indicate how the values of each preference variable are to be handled. In the TIRES data set, a ranking of 1 by a respondent indicates the most preferred combination of attribute values, while a ranking of 18 indicates the least preferred combination. When the smallest rank value corresponds to the most preferred combination of attribute values, the preference variable should be *reflected*, so high utility corresponds to high preference. The Market Research Application offers both metric and nonmetric conjoint analysis. The metric analysis uses the actual ranks, while the nonmetric analysis performs a monotone transformation of the ranks. Metric conjoint analysis requires the estimation of fewer parameters than nonmetric conjoint analysis, and it is the most commonly used type of conjoint analysis. For

*To update the examples provided with the software in Release 6.12, please see the section "Updating Samples for Release 6.12" on page 54.

this example, **Metric (reflected)** is suggested for each of the preference variables. Use the following steps to define the preference variables:

1. In the **Preferences** region, click the down arrow button and choose **Metric (reflected)** from the drop-down list.
2. In the **Variables** list box, select the variables JUDGE1, JUDGE2, ..., JUDGE7 by clicking on JUDGE1 and dragging down the list to JUDGE7.
3. In the **Variable Roles** region, click the [Preference] button.

You can define the attribute variables for the analysis in a manner similar to the one that is described for defining preference variables. You must define a measurement type for each attribute variable. In this example, all four attributes are regarded as qualitative, which is the default for the application.

Select the variables BRAND, CHARGES, PRICE, and MILEAGE from the **Variables** list box and click the [Attribute] button to define these variables as qualitative. You can remove any variable from its defined role by either selecting its name and clicking the [Remove] button or double-clicking its name in the appropriate list box.

If your data set contains an identification variable, specify that variable by selecting it in the **Variables** list box and clicking the [Id] button. The name of the variable then appears in the **Id** box. An Id variable must be a character variable, and it should indicate the combination of attribute levels for each observation.

A frequency is never used in individual-level variables in conjoint analysis. However, if you have an aggregate data set that includes a frequency variable, you should specify that variable by selecting it in the **Variables** list box and clicking the [Frequency] button. The name of the variable then appears in the **Frequency** box. The value of the frequency variable for an observation determines how many times that observation appears in the data.

A weight variable in a conjoint analysis distinguishes ordinary (active) observations, *holdouts* (products rated by the subjects but not used for model fitting), and simulation observations. For example, you can assign a value of 1 to active observations, a value of 0 to holdout observations, and a value of -1 to simulation observations. If you have no holdout observations and no simulated observations, then a weight variable is not required.

You can change the maximum number of iterations and convergence criteria for the analysis by clicking the [Iterations] button. To clear all selected variables and return all options to their default values, click the [Reset] button. To cancel all selections and return to the previous window, click the [Cancel] button. You can click the [Help] button at any time to view helpful information about the elements of this particular window.

After you have correctly defined all variable roles, click the [OK] button to proceed with the analysis. Once the analysis is complete, you can click the [Variables] button to return to the Conjoint Analysis Variable Selection window and change the model.

Accessing the Analysis Results

The Market Research Application provides a box-and-whisker plot of the relative importance of each attribute. The plot illustrates the variability of relative importance among respondents for each attribute. *Relative importance* is a measure of the importance of each attribute to the overall preference of a respondent; it is calculated for each respondent by dividing the range of utilities for each attribute by the sum of the utility ranges for all attributes and multiplying by 100.

In this example, MILEAGE is the most important attribute, with an average relative importance of 49%. The box-and-whisker plot displays the first and third quartiles as the ends of the box, the maximum and minimum as the whiskers (if they fall outside the box), and the median as a vertical bar in the interior of each box.

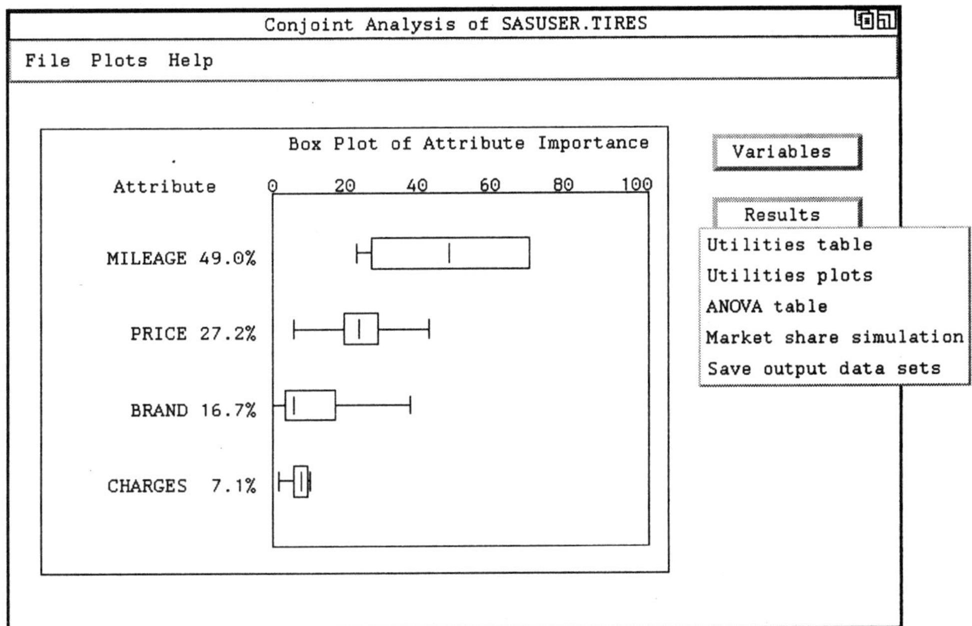

Figure 3. Plot of Relative Importance of Attributes

You can access analysis results by clicking the Results button on the conjoint analysis window. The following options are available:

- Utilities table
- Utilities plots
- ANOVA table
- Market share simulation
- Save output data sets

The Utilities Table

The Utilities Table window (Figure 4) displays the utility coefficients for each level of an attribute for all preferences (the dependent variables). The relative importance of each attribute is displayed separately for each preference variable (respondent).

The utilities table for this analysis indicates that BRAND is the most important attribute for JUDGE1, the first respondent, and that RollsAhead is the most preferred brand because it has the highest utility coefficient value. Thus, the first respondent preferred an 80,000-mile, $45.00 RollsAhead with no installation charge.

Utility Coefficients

File Help

Preference	Attribute	Relative Importance	Level	Utility
JUDGE1	BRAND	69.23	GoodTrea	0.0000
			RollsAhe	6.0000
			TireMax	-6.0000
	CHARGES	1.92	0	0.1667
			7.5	-0.1667
	PRICE	5.77	45	0.5000
			60	-0.0000
			75	-0.5000
	MILEAGE	23.08	40000	-2.0000
			60000	0.0000
			80000	2.0000
JUDGE2	BRAND	17.38	GoodTrea	1.8333
			RollsAhe	-1.3333
			TireMax	-0.5000
	CHARGES	10.37	0	0.9444
			7.5	-0.9444
	PRICE	23.78	45	1.0000
			60	1.6667
			75	-2.6667

Figure 4. Utility Table from Conjoint Analysis

Select Close from the File menu to close this window.

The Utilities Plots

To view the utilities in graphical form, click the Results button on the Conjoint Analysis window and select Utilities Plots from the pop-up menu. Figure 5 displays the resulting plots. To view the plot of the utilities for an attribute, click the name of the attribute in the Attribute list box on the right. The plot of the BRAND utilities indicates that one respondent clearly prefers RollsAhead; the line for that respondent shows a peak at RollsAhead, signifying high utility (preference). The other respondents only mildly prefer one brand over another.

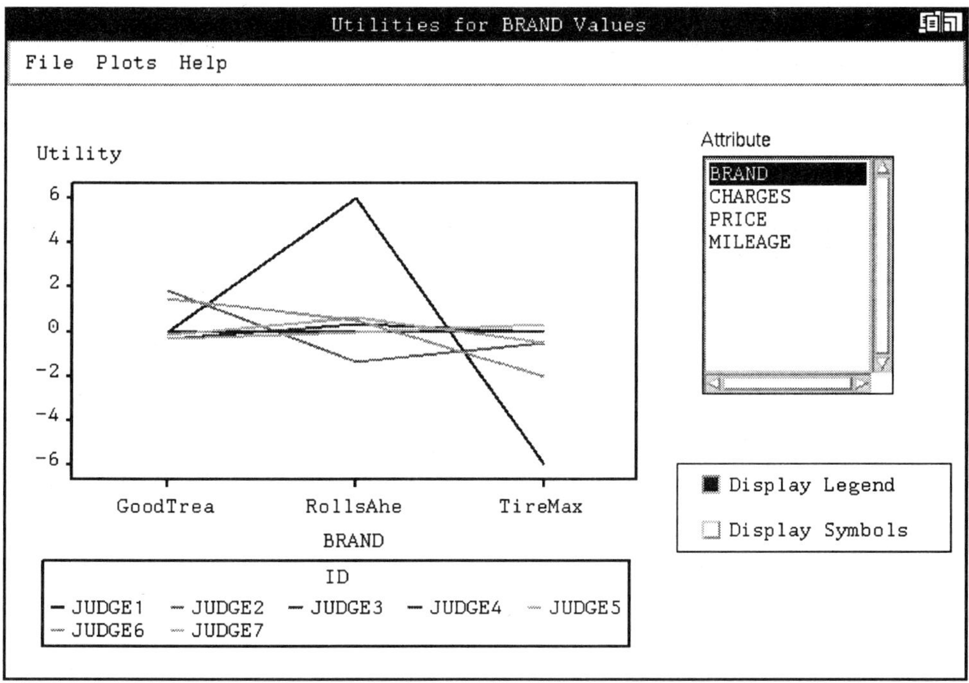

Figure 5. Utility Plot for BRAND

The ANOVA Table

To produce a standard ANOVA for each subject, click the Results button on the conjoint analysis window and select ANOVA table from the pop-up menu. Each preference variable and its associated transformation are listed in the Preference column. The F column displays the standard *F*-ratio for each preference variable, and the DF column displays the model and error degrees of freedom on which the *F*-ratio is based. The Par>F column lists the *p*-value for the overall fit of the conjoint analysis model to each subject, and the Adjusted R-square column lists the adjusted R-square statistic for the model that is fit to each subject. The Adjusted R-square statistic provides a rough indication of the fit of the conjoint analysis model. The R-square values range from 0 to 1, with a value near 1 indicating that the model adequately explains the variation in the responses. A low value of R-square may indicate either that there is an error in the data for that respondent or that the subject rated the choices inconsistently.

Note: The standard ANOVA assumptions are not met in conjoint analysis, so the results are, at best, approximate.

File Help

Univariate ANOVA Table Based on the Usual Degrees of Freedom

Preference		F	DF	Pr > F	Adjusted R-square
JUDGE1	Metric	690.71	7,10	0.0001	0.996
JUDGE2	Metric	4.13	7,10	0.0216	0.563
JUDGE3	Metric	29.41	7,10	0.0001	0.921
JUDGE4	Metric	10000.00	7,10	0.0001	1.000
JUDGE5	Metric	45.41	7,10	0.0001	0.948
JUDGE6	Metric	25.19	7,10	0.0001	0.909
JUDGE7	Metric	72.73	7,10	0.0001	0.967

Figure 6. ANOVA Table from Conjoint Analysis

Market Share Simulation

To perform market share simulation, click the Results button and select Market share simulation from the pop-up menu. You can calculate the expected market share for product by using one of three simulation models: maximum utility, logit, or Bradley-Terry-Luce. The maximum utility simulation model is the default. The three models are described in more detail in SAS Technical Report R-109, *Conjoint Analysis Examples*, pages 3, 56, 57, and 58.

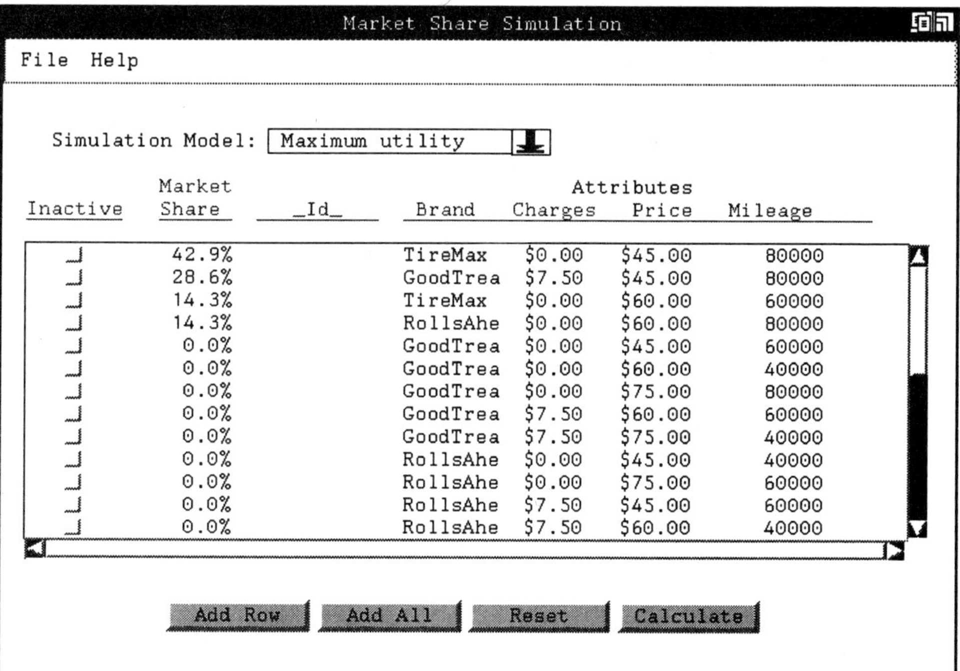

Figure 7. Market Share Simulation

The entry in the table with the largest market share is the 80,000-mile, $45.00 TireMax with no installation charge. It is expected to account for 42.9% of the market under the maximum utility simulation model. You can select the logit model and the Bradley-Terry-Luce model by clicking the down arrow to the right of the Simulation Model box. Selecting a model from this drop-down list automatically recalculates the estimated market shares. The three models available for market share simulation usually produce different answers. The maximum utility model is the most commonly used of the three models.

Only 18 of the 54 possible tire purchase combinations are presented to the respondents. You may want to predict the expected market share of one or more of the combinations that are not present in the sample. To add a single row, follow these steps (see Figure 8):

1. Click the Add Row button at the bottom of the window; this adds a row at the top of the table.
2. Click -Select- to select values for each variable from the pop-up menu that appears. You can also edit the Id column.

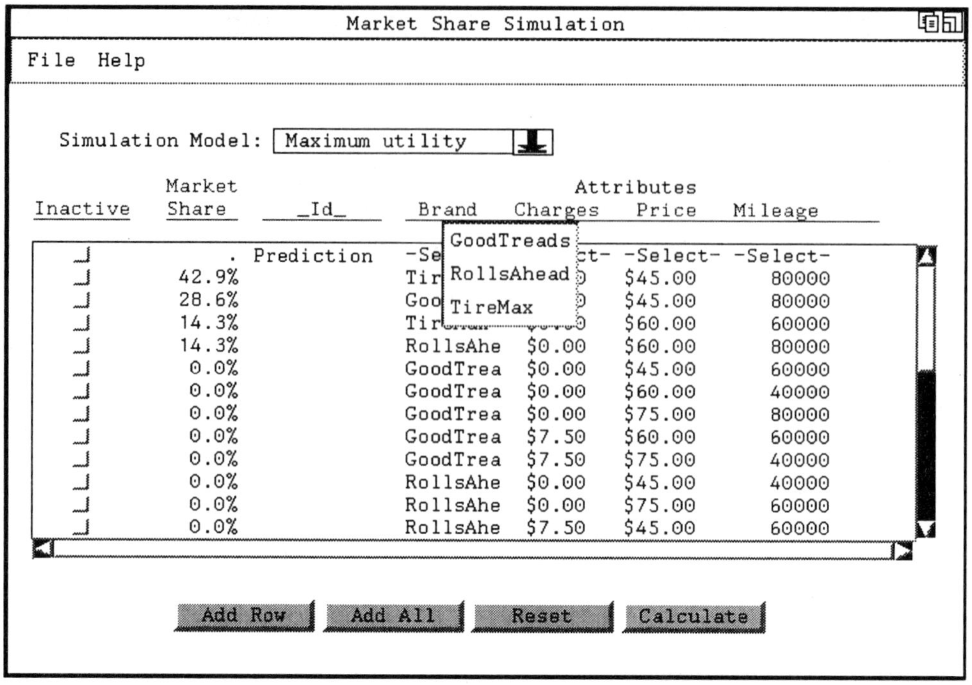

Market Share Simulation

File Help

Simulation Model: Maximum utility

Inactive	Market Share	_Id_	Brand	Charges	Price	Mileage
	.	Prediction	-Se	ct-	-Select-	-Select-
	42.9%		Tir		$45.00	80000
	28.6%		Goo		$45.00	80000
	14.3%		Tir		$60.00	60000
	14.3%		RollsAhe	$0.00	$60.00	80000
	0.0%		GoodTrea	$0.00	$45.00	60000
	0.0%		GoodTrea	$0.00	$60.00	40000
	0.0%		GoodTrea	$0.00	$75.00	80000
	0.0%		GoodTrea	$7.50	$60.00	60000
	0.0%		GoodTrea	$7.50	$75.00	40000
	0.0%		RollsAhe	$0.00	$45.00	40000
	0.0%		RollsAhe	$0.00	$75.00	60000
	0.0%		RollsAhe	$7.50	$45.00	60000

GoodTreads
RollsAhead
TireMax

Add Row | Add All | Reset | Calculate

Figure 8. Adding a Row to a Market Share Simulation

You can add as many rows as you want, then click the Calculate button to rerun the simulation. You can also include all possible combinations in the table by clicking the Add All button. If you create a duplicate observation, a warning message displays. After any calculation, you can restore the original sample by clicking Reset and Calculate in sequence.

Figure 9 displays the results of adding a row for the combination of RollsAhead brand, no installation charge, $45.00 purchase price, and an expected tread mileage of 80,000 miles and then recalculating the simulation using the maximum utility model. A market share of 64.3% is estimated for the newly added combination. The combination that previously had the largest market share has dropped to only a 7.1% market share with the introduction of this new purchasing option. Thus, you expect an 80,000-mile, $45.00 RollsAhead tire with no installation charge to do well if introduced into the current market represented by the 18 tire purchase alternatives presented to the respondents.

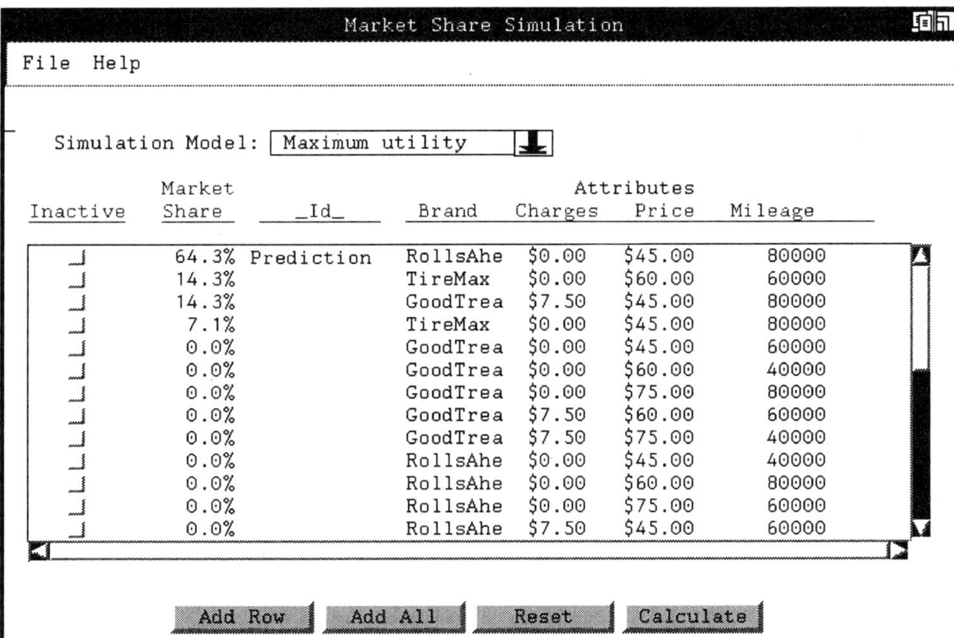

Figure 9. Market Share Prediction

You can exclude any row from further simulations by clicking the corresponding box in the Inactive column. The box in the Inactive column is colored black when that row is inactive. Inactive rows appear at the bottom of the table after a simulation has been calculated. Clicking again in the Inactive box includes that row in future simulations.

Saving the Output Data Sets

You can save the data sets that you created for the conjoint analysis by clicking the Results button in the conjoint analysis window and selecting Save output data sets. These data sets include the computed utility and importance scores, as well as the transformations and resulting scores.

Performing New Analyses

To redo the same analysis with the same data set but with different options, click the Variables button in the conjoint analysis window (Figure 3) to return to the variable selection window (Figure 2).

To start a new analysis, select File from the menu bar on the conjoint analysis window, and then select New data set/analysis. Each time you change the data set or analysis or exit the application, you are asked if you want to save the changes that you have made during the session. The File menu also contains items for saving and printing the analysis. To quit the Market Research Application, select End from the File menu.

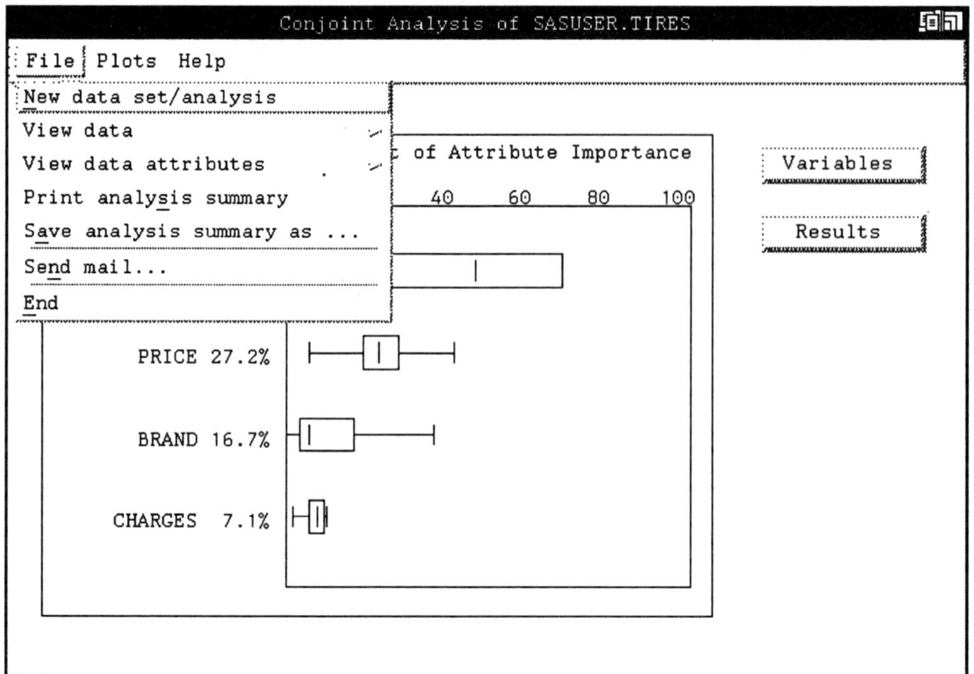

Figure 10. Beginning a New Analysis

References

Green, P.E., and Srinivasan, V. (1990), "Conjoint Analysis in Marketing: New Developments with Implications for Research and Practice," *Journal of Marketing*, 54, 3–19.

Louviere, J.J. (1988), *Analyzing Decision Making, Metric Conjoint Analysis*, Sage University Papers, Beverly Hills, CA: Sage Publications.

SAS Institute Inc. (1996), *Marketing Research: Practical Applications Using the SAS System Course Notes*, Cary, NC: SAS Institute Inc.

SAS Institute Inc. (1993), SAS Technical Report R-109, *Conjoint Analysis Examples*, Cary, NC: SAS Institute Inc.

Correspondence Analysis

Researchers collected information on subjects and their cars. Each individual provided information about the country of origin of their car (ORIGIN), the size of their car (SIZE), the type of their car (TYPE), whether they rent or own their home (HOME), the number of incomes in their home (NINCOME), their marital status (NMARITAL), their gender (SEX), and the number of children at home. This information is included in the CARS sample data set.

The goal in correspondence analysis is to determine the relationships among variables. Simple correspondence analysis is used when you are investigating the crosstabulations between two specific sets of variables. Multiple correspondence analysis is used to investigate all possible pairs of crosstabulations of a set of variables.

Note: This analysis is also described in the chapter for the CORRESP procedure in the latest version of the *SAS/STAT User's Guide.*

Selecting the Input Data Set

The input data set may be either the raw variable values or a specific contingency table. The CARS data set consists of raw data. The following DATA step creates the data set CARS:

```
data cars;
   input origin $ size $ type $ home $ sex $ nincome
         marital;
   if nincome=1 then income='1 Income ';
   else              income='2 Incomes';
   if nmarital=0       then marital='Single        ';
   else if nmarital=1  then marital='Married       ';
   else if nmarital=10 then marital='Single w Kids ';
   else                     marital='Married w Kids';
   datalines;
American Large  Family Own  Male   1 11
Japanese Small  Sporty Own  Male   1 00
Japanese Small  Family Own  Male   2 01
American Large  Family Rent Male   1 00
American Medium Family Own  Male   2 11
European Medium Family Own  Female 2 11
...[333 other records]
;
```

The data can also be input in the form of a contingency table. For example, if you want to analyze the relationship between ORIGIN and MARITAL, you can create the following contingency table as input:

```
data cars2;
   input marital $14. American European Japanese;
   datalines;
Single          33 15 63
Married         37 14 51
Single w Kids    6  1  8
Married w Kids  52 15 44
;
```

Defining the Variables

You can specify the type of analysis you want to perform in the Correspondence Analysis Variable Selection window (Figure 11). The default selections in this window are Simple Correspondence Analysis and Raw Variables.

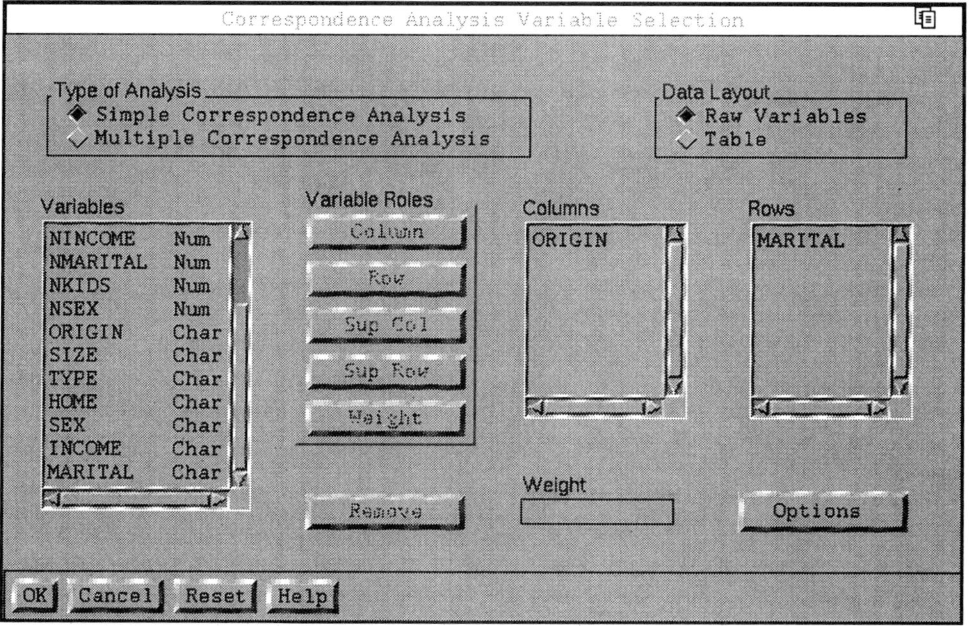

Figure 11. Simple Correspondence Analysis Variable Selection

Since the CARS data set consists of the raw values of the variables, use the default selection Raw Variables in the Data Layout box. (If the data are in contingency table form, you select Table.) To specify variables for the columns and rows, click the Column and Row buttons, respectively. The analysis is based on the contingency table created from these variables. You can specify a weight variable for each observation by clicking the Weight button. Observations with a weight greater than 0 are included in the analysis. Click the Sup Col and Sup Row buttons to specify supplementary columns and rows, respectively. Supplementary columns and rows are not used in the analysis, but they are projected onto the plot. Click the Remove button to remove a variable from its assigned role in the analysis. Clicking the Options button displays the window shown in Figure 12.

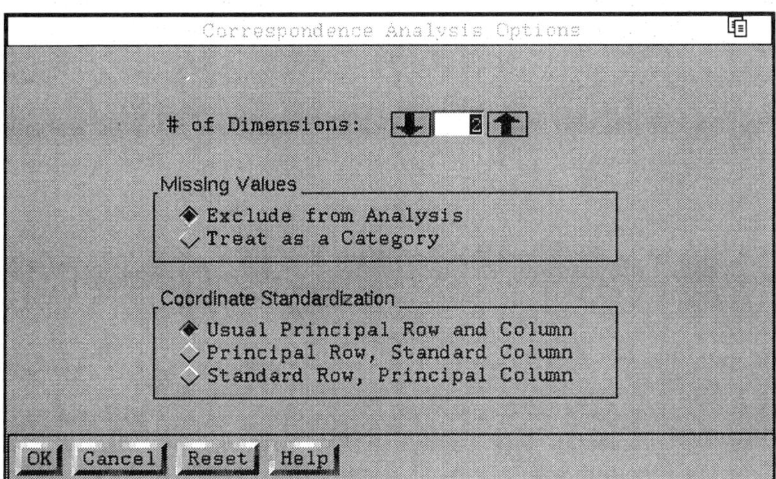

Figure 12. Correspondence Analysis Options

In the Correspondence Analysis Options window, you can change the number of dimensions used in the analysis either by clicking the up and down arrows in the # of Dimensions box or by entering a value in this box. You can also indicate how you want missing values treated and what type of coordinate standardization you prefer. To cancel your selections and return to the previous window, click the Cancel button; to clear your selections and return this window to the default selections, click the Reset button. To save your changes and return to the variable selection window, click the OK button. You can click the Help button at any time to receive help on any of the items in this window.

Accessing the Analysis Results

Simple Correspondence Analysis

The next step investigates the relationship between the variables ORIGIN and MARITAL. The variable ORIGIN has three values: American, Japanese, and European. The variable MARITAL has four values: Single, Single with Kids, Married, and Married with Kids. The default analysis in the variable selection window is a simple correspondence analysis that uses raw data. To make ORIGIN the column variable, select ORIGIN from the Variables list box on the Correspondence Analysis Variable Selection window, and then click the Column button under Variable Roles. Next, select MARITAL from the Variables list box and click the Row button to make MARITAL the row variable. Click the OK button to perform the analysis.

Figure 13 displays the correspondence analysis window. It displays a plot of the column points and the row points of the table. A simple correspondence plot should be viewed as two separate plots overlaid, one for the column points and one for the row points. Distances between column and row points have no meaning, but distances between row points and other row points and distances between column points and other column points do indicate similar profiles. Interpreting a simple correspondence plot involves three steps:

1. Examine the column points for clustering. Column points that are close together have similar column profiles.
2. Examine the row points for clustering. Row points that are close together have similar row profiles.
3. Compare the column points to the row points. Column and row points that lie in roughly the same direction away from the origin and in roughly the same region of space are associated with each other.

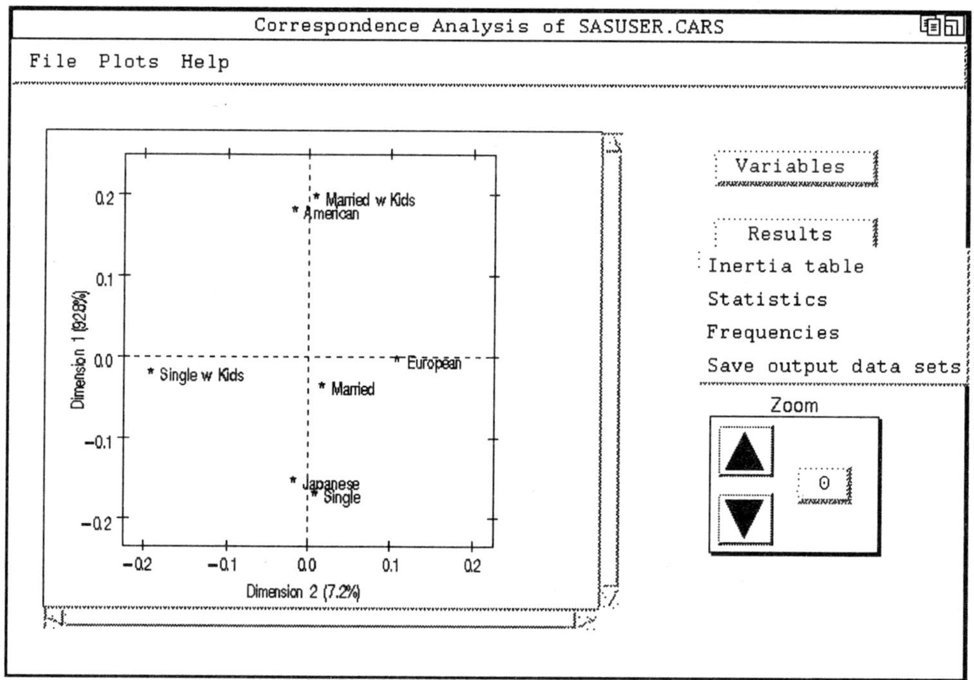

Figure 13. Simple Correspondence Analysis Plot

There appears to be no clustering of ORIGIN points, so each country of origin is associated with a different category of the variable MARITAL. The MARITAL points also show no clustering. The values American and Married with Kids are both in the same direction away from the point (0,0) and are both in the same region of the plot; this indicates that more people who are married with kids drive American cars than would be expected if ORIGIN and MARITAL were independent. Similarly, more single people drive Japanese cars than would be expected if ORIGIN and MARITAL were independent; the points for the values Japanese and Single are both in the same direction from (0,0), and they lie in the same region of the plot.

The plot magnification is determined by the controls in the Zoom box. Clicking the up arrow button increases the magnification, and clicking the down arrow button decreases the magnification. Clicking the [0] button resets the plot to its original size. If you increase the magnification, you can use the horizontal and vertical scroll bars that surround the plot to view all regions of the plot.

Click the [Results] button to view the following analysis results:

- Inertia table
- Statistics
- Frequencies
- Save output data sets

The Inertia table is displayed in Figure 14. This table lists the singular values and inertias for all possible dimensions in the analysis. A simple correspondence analysis plot attempts to summarize and display the information contained in a contingency table. *Inertia* is a measure of how well the correspondence analysis approximates the column and row profiles of the contingency table. The first dimension of the plot (the first row of the table) accounts for 92.84% of the total inertia, and the second dimension accounts for 7.16% of the total inertia. Thus, the two-dimensional plot characterizes the information in the contingency table completely. When this total is less than 100%, more dimensions may be useful in improving the analysis results.

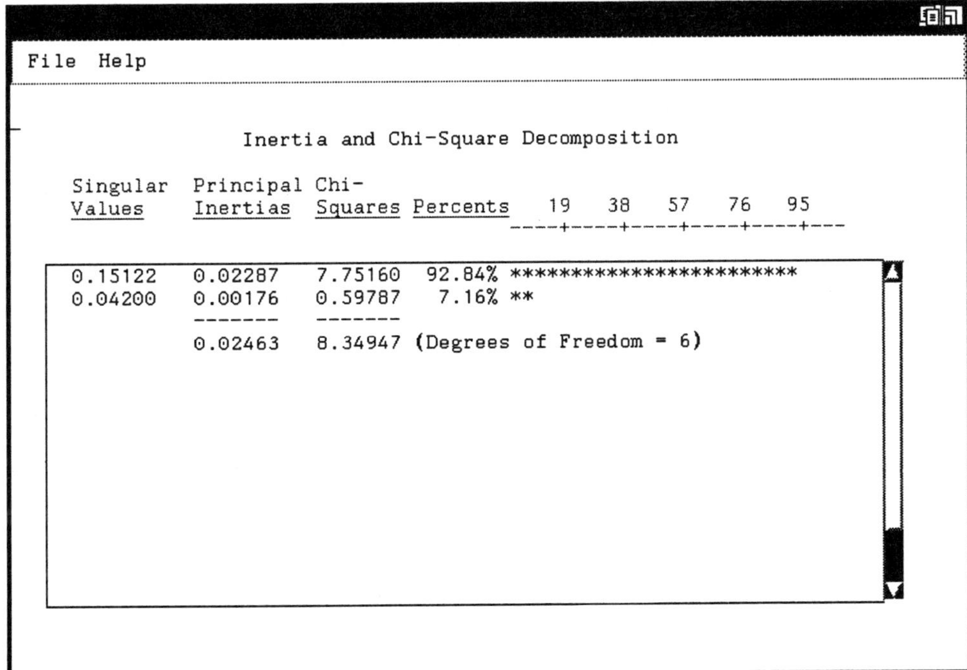

File Help

Inertia and Chi-Square Decomposition

```
Singular  Principal Chi-
Values    Inertias  Squares Percents   19    38    57    76    95
                                    ----+-----+-----+-----+-----+---
0.15122   0.02287   7.75160  92.84% ************************
0.04200   0.00176   0.59787   7.16% **
          -------   -------
          0.02463   8.34947 (Degrees of Freedom = 6)
```

Figure 14. Inertia Table from Simple Correspondence Analysis

The statistics window includes quality, mass, inertia, row and column coordinates, correlations (squared cosines), and the partial contributions to inertia for each variable for each dimension. To select different presentations of the statistics, click the Tables button.

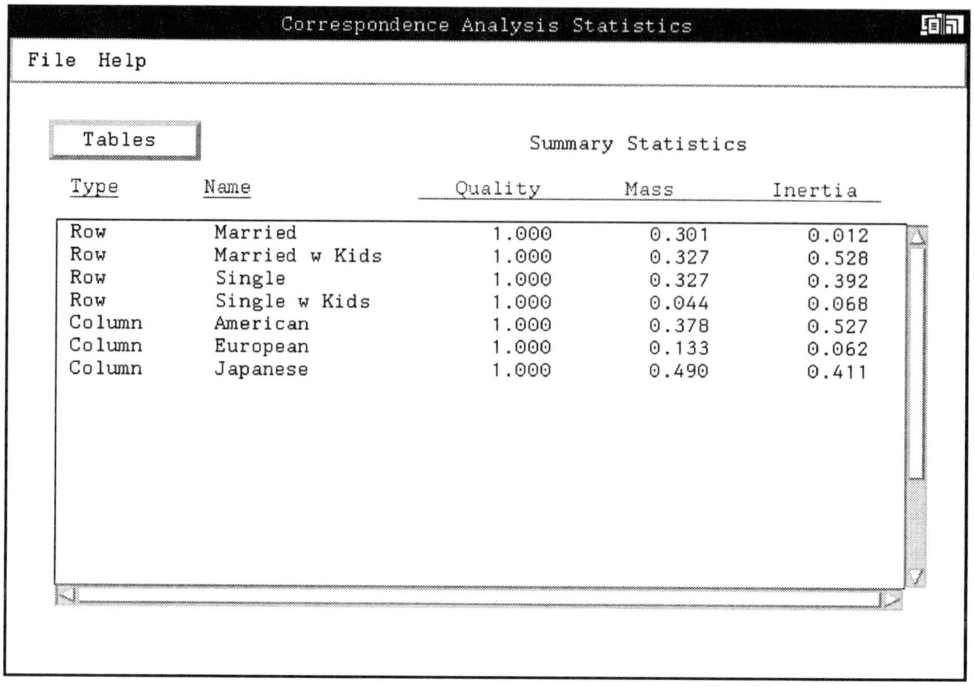

Correspondence Analysis Statistics

File Help

Tables

Summary Statistics

Type	Name	Quality	Mass	Inertia
Row	Married	1.000	0.301	0.012
Row	Married w Kids	1.000	0.327	0.528
Row	Single	1.000	0.327	0.392
Row	Single w Kids	1.000	0.044	0.068
Column	American	1.000	0.378	0.527
Column	European	1.000	0.133	0.062
Column	Japanese	1.000	0.490	0.411

Figure 15. Statistics from Simple Correspondence Analysis

The summary statistics (quality, mass, and inertia) are displayed for each variable. *Quality* is a measure of how well each row and column is represented by the number of dimensions used in the analysis. Quality values range from 0 to 1. In this example, all quality values are 1.000, which indicates that two dimensions completely represent all rows and all columns. If quality values are less than 1, then more dimensions are needed to completely represent that particular row or column. *Mass* is another term for marginal relative frequency. The row masses are the sums of the relative frequencies over all columns; the column masses are the sums of the relative frequencies over all rows.

Clicking on the Tables button produces the pop-up menu shown in Figure 16. From this menu, you can choose to display the coordinates, the squared cosines (correlations), or the partial contributions (to inertia) for each variable for each dimension.

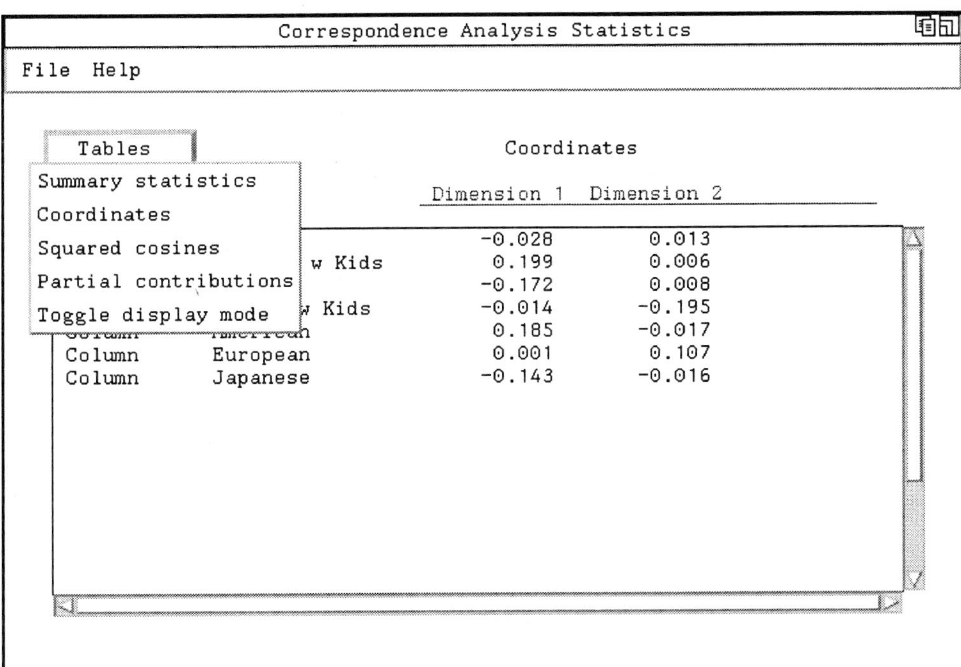

Figure 16. Tables Pop-Up Menu

If you select **Toggle display mode** from the pop-up menu, the display format changes so that coordinates, correlations, and contributions are displayed together for each dimension for each variable (see Figure 17).

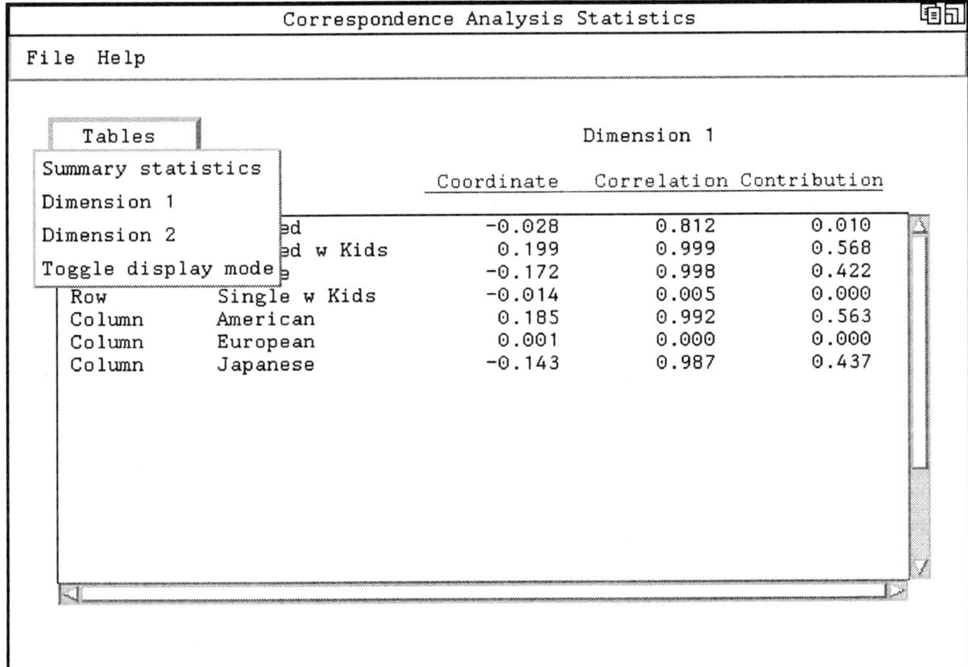

Figure 17. Toggle Display Mode

The frequencies window includes the observed contingency table, the expected contingency table, the table of deviations (observed minus expected), and the cell chi-squares, as well as row and column profile tables. You can display the different tables by clicking the Tables button. The deviations table is shown in Figure 18. You can confirm the interpretation of the correspondence analysis plot (shown in Figure 13 on page 22) by inspecting the deviations. The Married w Kids row indicates that there are more American cars than were expected (and fewer Japanese cars than were expected) belonging to owners who are married with kids. The Single row indicates that there are more Japanese cars than were expected (and fewer American cars than were expected) belonging to owners who are single without kids.

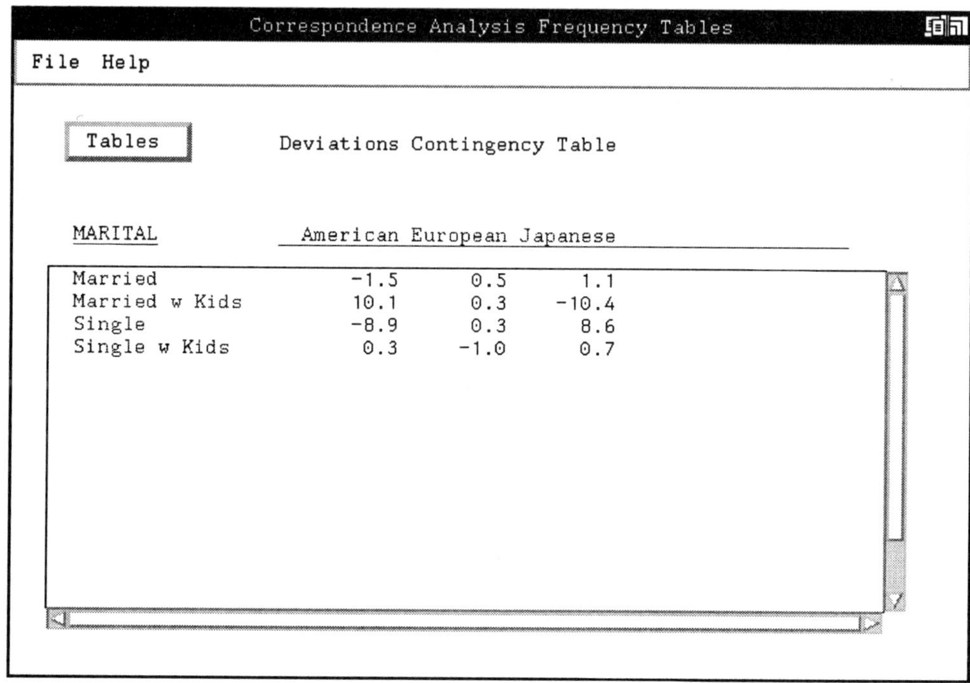

Figure 18. Frequencies from Simple Correspondence Analysis

To save the coordinates used in the plot as a data set, click the Results button in the correspondence analysis window (shown in Figure 13 on page 22) and select Save output data sets.

Multiple Correspondence Analysis

A multiple correspondence analysis is also appropriate for these data. To perform an analysis with the variables ORIGIN, TYPE, SIZE, HOME, SEX, INCOME, and MARITAL, follow these steps:

1. Click the Variables button in the correspondence analysis window to return to the Correspondence Analysis Variable Selection window.
2. Remove the current column and row variables either by double-clicking on them or by selecting them and clicking the Remove button. Clicking the Reset button also removes all current variables and returns all other options to their defaults.
3. Select Multiple Correspondence Analysis in the Type of Analysis box in the upper left of the window.
4. Select the column variables ORIGIN, SIZE, TYPE, HOME, SEX, INCOME, and MARITAL by clicking on the ORIGIN variable and dragging through the list to the MARITAL variable, and then clicking the Column button.

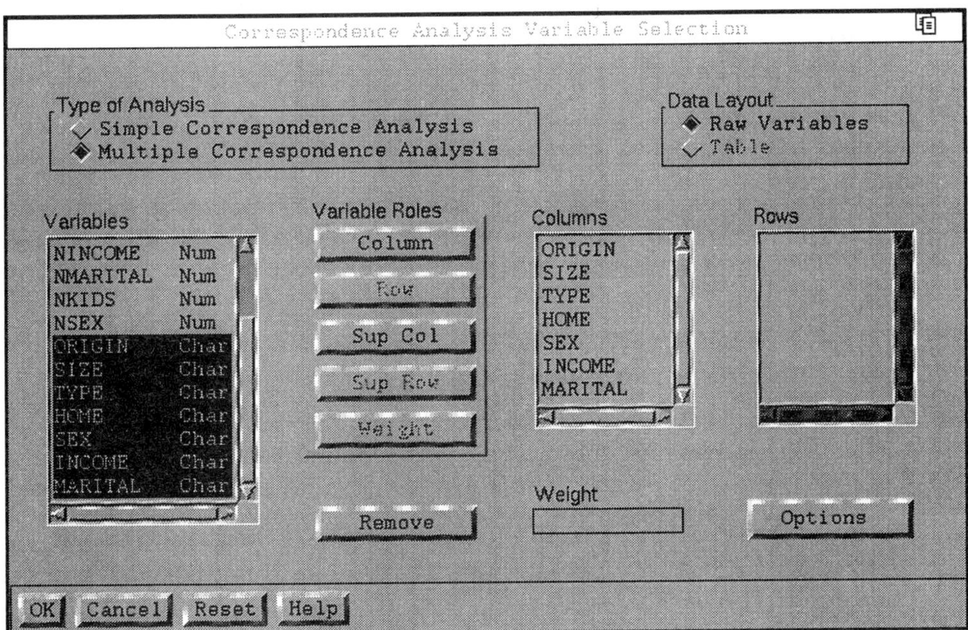

Figure 19. Multiple Correspondence Analysis Variable Selection

5. Click the Options button and increase the number of dimensions to three (or more) by clicking the up arrow button in the options dialog box that appears.
6. Click the OK button in the options dialog and click the OK button in the variables selection window to perform the analysis.

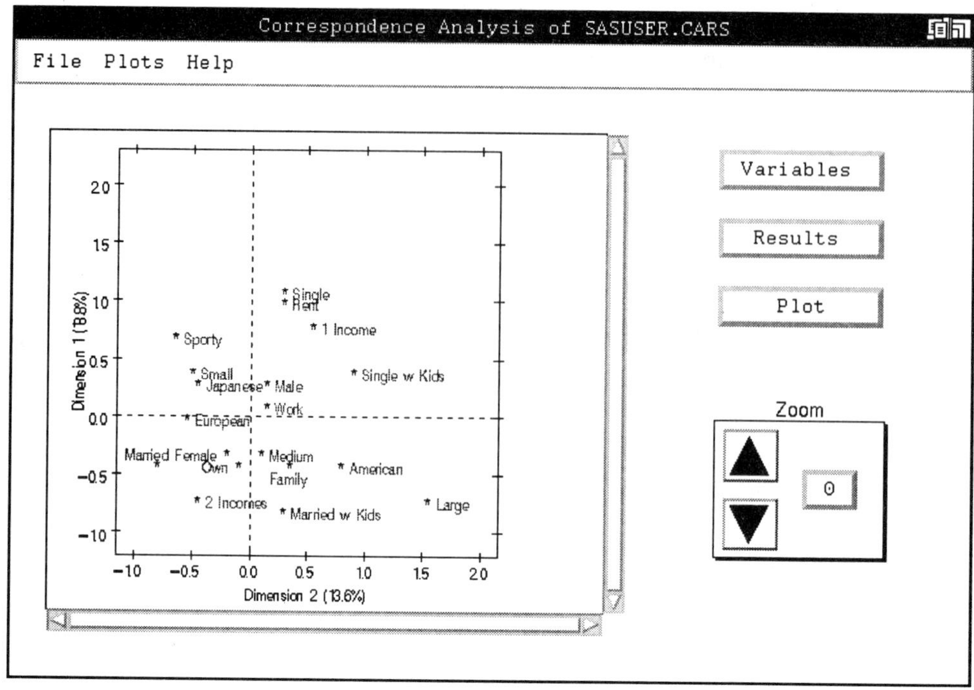

Figure 20. Multiple Correspondence Analysis Plot

The correspondence analysis window displays a plot of the levels of each variable (Figure 20). The variable SIZE has the values Small, Medium, and Large; the variable TYPE has the values Family, Sporty, and Work vehicle; the variable HOME has the values Own and Rent; and the variable INCOME has the values 1 Income and 2 Incomes. Interpreting a multiple correspondence analysis plot is more difficult than interpreting a simple correspondence analysis plot because none of the distances between points have any straightforward meaning. There are two guidelines to keep in mind when interpreting a multiple correspondence analysis plot:

- Levels of the same variable that lie in approximately the same direction away from the origin and in approximately the same region of the plot have similar frequency distributions relative to the other variables.
- Levels of different variables that lie in approximately the same direction away from the origin and in approximately the same region of the plot are associated with each other.

By following these guidelines, you can conclude that

- Single, Rent, and 1 Income are associated
- Sporty, Small, and Japanese are associated
- Married and 2 Incomes are associated
- Married with Kids, Large, American, and Family are associated

You can use this type of information to determine the proper target audience for certain marketing strategies and advertising. You can view the same results for multiple correspondence analysis as for simple correspondence analysis by clicking the Results button.

When more than two dimensions have been analyzed, you can click the Plot button to select which two dimensions are displayed in the plot (Figure 21).

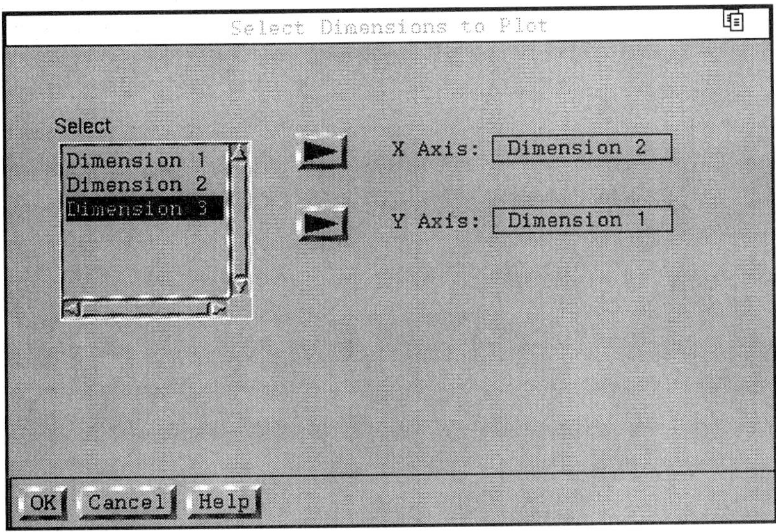

Figure 21. Select Dimensions to Plot

For example, select Dimension 3 from the Select list box and click on the right arrow button to the left of the Y Axis label to assign Dimension 3 to the vertical axis of the plot. Click the OK button to display the new plot.

Performing New Analyses

To redo the same analysis with the same data set but different options, click the Variables button on the correspondence analysis window to return to the variable selection window. To start a new analysis, select File from the menu bar, and select New data set/analysis from the File menu. Each time you change the data set or analysis or exit the application, you are asked if you want to save the changes that you have made during the session.

References

Greenacre, M.J. (1984), *Theory and Applications of Correspondence Analysis*, London: Academic Press.

Greenacre, M.J. and Hastie, T. (1987), "The Geometric Interpretation of Correspondence Analysis," *Journal of the American Statistical Association*, 82, 437–447.

Hoffman, D.L. and Franke, G.R. (1986), "Correspondence Analysis: Graphical Representation of Categorical Data in Marketing Research," *Journal of Marketing Research*, 23, 213–227.

SAS Institute Inc. (1996), *Marketing Research: Practical Applications Using the SAS System Course Notes*, Cary, NC: SAS Institute Inc.

SAS Institute Inc. (1989), *SAS/STAT User's Guide, Volume 1, Version 6, Fourth Edition,* Cary, NC: SAS Institute Inc, 943.

Discrete Choice Analysis

Discrete choice analysis* is used to investigate consumers' choices of products defined by attributes. Attributes such as price and brand are called *choice attributes* because they are the variables that determine the specific choices that respondents are asked to make in the experiment.

In this example, eight choice sets, each with a different set of five combinations of price and brand, are presented to each respondent. The respondent selects one of the five alternatives from each choice set. The goal is to determine the market share of the various products.

Selecting the Input Data Set

The data from a choice experiment can be contained in either one or two data sets. When the data are contained in one data set, all alternatives must be present, as well as a variable that indicates which alternative each respondent chose. When the data are in two data sets, one data set must contain all the alternatives presented to the respondents, and the other data set must contain the responses (the chosen alternatives). In either case, you can use a frequency variable. If you use a frequency variable and the data are in two data sets, the frequency variable should be in the data set that contains the responses. The single data set format is used more commonly; it is discussed further in this section.

In the Select a Data Set and Analysis window (Figure 22), select SASUSER from the **Library** list box and then select PRICE Discrete Choice Analysis† in the **Data Set and Last Analysis** list box. Click the **OK** button to proceed with the analysis.

*Discrete choice analysis is sometimes referred to as *choice-based conjoint analysis.*

†To update the examples provided with the software in Release 6.12, please see the section "Updating Samples for Release 6.12" on page 54.

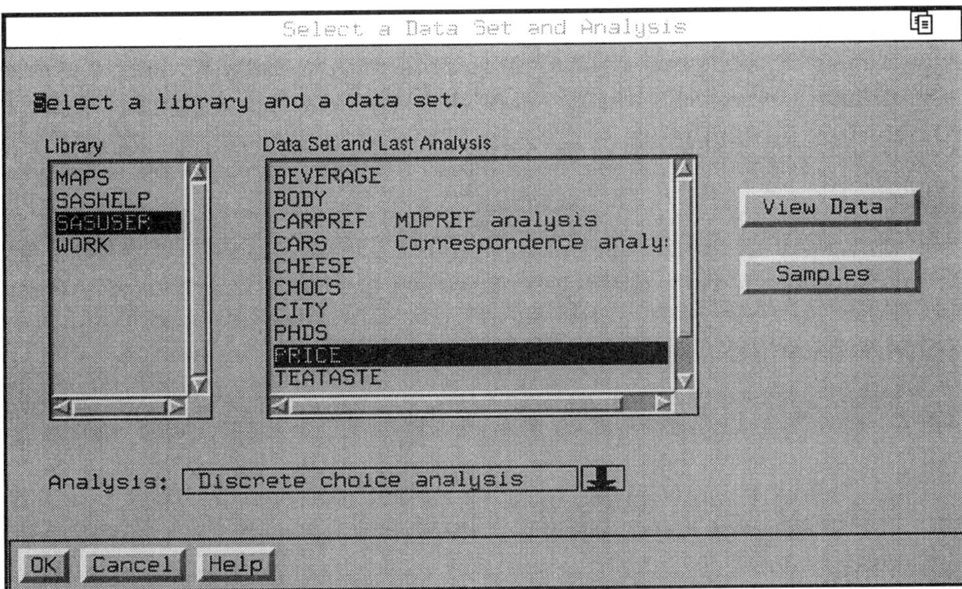

Figure 22. Select the PRICE Data Set for Discrete Choice Analysis

With the other analyses, you are taken directly to the appropriate variable selection window. With discrete choice analysis, a supplementary window is displayed to help you determine if your data are in the appropriate form. This supplementary window (shown in Figure 23) appears only the first time you select a data set for a discrete choice analysis.

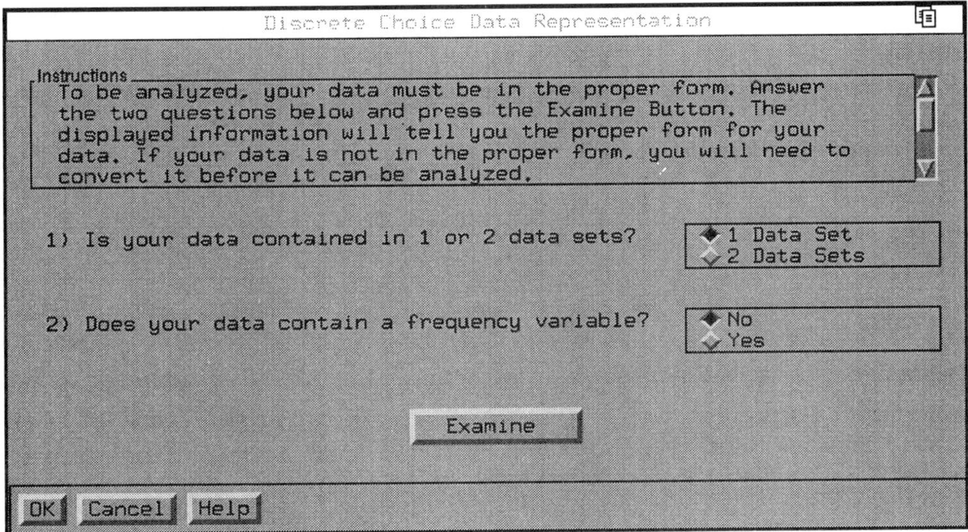

Figure 23. Discrete Choice Data Representation

The form of the input data is very important for discrete choice analysis. The PRICE data set contains both choice and response data but no frequency variable, so you should select **1 Data Set** and **No,** as shown in Figure 23. Note that clicking the Examine button displays some Help information about the required form of the input data.

The PRICE data set, several observations of which are displayed in Figure 24, has the proper form for one data set without a frequency variable. One observation is recorded for every choice alternative in the choice sets given to each subject. Since every respondent evaluates eight choice sets of five products, there are 40 observations recorded for each subject. The first five observations in Figure 24 contain the results of the first subject's response to the first choice set. The choice attribute BRAND, which has the values $1, 2, \ldots, 5$, must be represented as the five dummy variables BRAND1–BRAND5. These dummy variables and PRICE describe the presented choice alternatives, while the response variable C has the value 1 for the chosen alternative (in this case, Brand 2 at $5.99) and the value 2 otherwise (these are the unchosen alternatives, or the unobserved second or subsequent choices).

OBS	SUBJ	SET	BRAND1	BRAND2	BRAND3	BRAND4	BRAND5	PRICE	BRAND	C
1	1	1	1	0	0	0	0	5.99	1	2
2	1	1	0	1	0	0	0	5.99	2	1
3	1	1	0	0	1	0	0	5.99	3	2
4	1	1	0	0	0	1	0	5.99	4	2
5	1	1	0	0	0	0	1	4.99	5	2
6	1	2	1	0	0	0	0	5.99	1	2
7	1	2	0	1	0	0	0	5.99	2	1
8	1	2	0	0	1	0	0	3.99	3	2
9	1	2	0	0	0	1	0	3.99	4	2
10	1	2	0	0	0	0	1	4.99	5	2
11	1	3	1	0	0	0	0	5.99	1	2
12	1	3	0	1	0	0	0	3.99	2	2
13	1	3	0	0	1	0	0	5.99	3	1
14	1	3	0	0	0	1	0	3.99	4	2
15	1	3	0	0	0	0	1	4.99	5	2
16	1	4	1	0	0	0	0	5.99	1	1
17	1	4	0	1	0	0	0	3.99	2	2
18	1	4	0	0	1	0	0	3.99	3	2
19	1	4	0	0	0	1	0	5.99	4	2
20	1	4	0	0	0	0	1	4.99	5	2

Figure 24. Individual Level Data, First 20 Observations out of 4000

Alternatively, you may choose to aggregate your data over the individuals and include a frequency variable that contains the number of selections of a choice alternative within each choice set. For large data sets, you may increase computer performance by using aggregate data. This data set would contain both choice and response data and a frequency variable, so you would select **1 Data Set** and **Yes** in the Discrete Choice Representation window. The following statements create the aggregate data set shown in Figure 25.

```
proc summary data=sasuser.price nway;
   class set brand1-brand5 price c;
   output out=aggre(drop=_type_);
proc print data=aggre;
run;
```

OBS	SET	BRAND1	BRAND2	BRAND3	BRAND4	BRAND5	PRICE	C	_FREQ_
1	1	0	0	0	0	1	4.99	1	14
2	1	0	0	0	0	1	4.99	2	86
3	1	0	0	0	1	0	5.99	1	33
4	1	0	0	0	1	0	5.99	2	67
5	1	0	0	1	0	0	5.99	1	22
6	1	0	0	1	0	0	5.99	2	78
7	1	0	1	0	0	0	5.99	1	19
8	1	0	1	0	0	0	5.99	2	81
9	1	1	0	0	0	0	5.99	1	12
10	1	1	0	0	0	0	5.99	2	88
11	2	0	0	0	0	1	4.99	1	5
12	2	0	0	0	0	1	4.99	2	95
13	2	0	0	0	1	0	3.99	1	27
14	2	0	0	0	1	0	3.99	2	73
15	2	0	0	1	0	0	3.99	1	8
16	2	0	0	1	0	0	3.99	2	92
17	2	0	1	0	0	0	5.99	1	26
18	2	0	1	0	0	0	5.99	2	74
19	2	1	0	0	0	0	5.99	1	34
20	2	1	0	0	0	0	5.99	2	66

Figure 25. Aggregate Data, First 20 Observations out of 80

In the aggregate data set (Figure 25), two observations are recorded for each choice alternative in each choice set. The aggregate data set for this example has 80 observations since there are eight choice sets each with five alternatives. The first two records show that 14 of the respondents chose Brand 5 from the first choice set, while 86 made different choices; the first ten records contain all of the aggregate information on the first choice set.

Variable selection and discrete choice analysis of the individual level data is described in the following sections. An analysis with the aggregate data proceeds similarly, and the results obtained are the same.

Defining the Variables

In the Discrete Choice Analysis Variable Selection window (Figure 26), select several required variables: a response variable, some choice attribute variables, and a subject variable. Optionally, you can also choose a frequency variable and some non-choice attribute variables. If you select a frequency variable, a subject variable is not necessary.

In this example, C is the response variable. Select C from the Variables list and click the Response button. You must indicate which value of the response variable represents a choice. Clicking on the down arrow button to the right of the Choice Event box displays a drop-down list of the different values of the variable C. In this example, the value 1 indicates the chosen alternative and the value 2 indicates the nonchosen alternatives, so choose the value 1.

Next, specify PRICE, BRAND1, BRAND2, BRAND3, BRAND4, and BRAND5 as choice attributes by selecting them from the **Variables** list and clicking the **Choice** button in the **Variable Roles** region. Originally, BRAND was a categorical variable with five levels that represent the five different brands being considered. Here, it is represented as five dummy variables.* Note that you can omit the variable BRAND5 from the analysis because its parameters are zero (because the other four dummy variables uniquely determine the value of BRAND5); however, including all five dummy variables can help identify model specification problems.

You must also declare a variable that distinguishes the choice sets. The choice set variable in this example is SET; you should select SET from the **Variables** list and click the **Choice Set** button. The variable SET has the values $1, 2, \ldots, 8$ for the eight different choice sets. Choice probabilities are estimated separately for each choice set. Non-choice attributes are independent variables like the choice attributes, but non-choice attributes pertain to the subjects not the products. Non-choice attributes should be crossed with choice attributes in the data set. For example, if you have a non-choice attribute (AGE) in addition to the choice attribute (PRICE), and a categorical choice attribute (BRAND) represented by five dummy variables (BRAND1–BRAND5), then AGE should be represented in the data set as six variables: AGE*PRICE, AGE*BRAND1, ... , and AGE*BRAND5. The estimated parameters for BRAND5 and AGE*BRAND5 should be 0.

A subject ID variable distinguishes different respondents or groups of respondents. A subject ID variable is required only if you do not have a frequency variable in your data set. Select SUBJ from the **Variables** list and click the **Subject** button to assign it as the subject variable.

After you select the appropriate variables, click the **OK** button to perform the analysis. Clicking the **Help** button produces help specific to this window, and clicking the **Reset** button clears all variable roles.

*Each dummy variable has the value of 1 for a different level of the attribute. In this way, each dummy variable represents the presence of that level and the absence of the other levels.

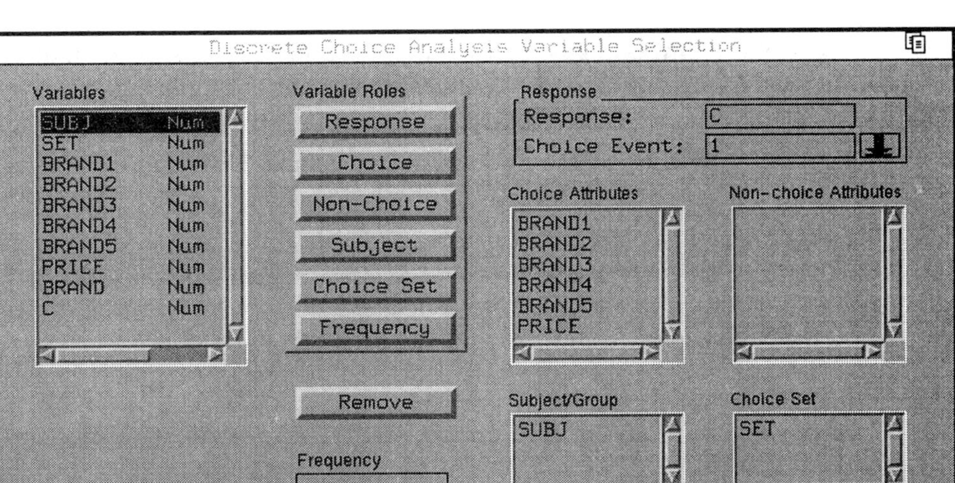

Figure 26. Discrete Choice Analysis Variable Selection

Accessing the Analysis Results

The discrete choice analysis window displays a bar chart of the significances of each of the choice and non-choice attributes. In Figure 27, the chart indicates that PRICE, BRAND1, BRAND2, and BRAND4 are significant.

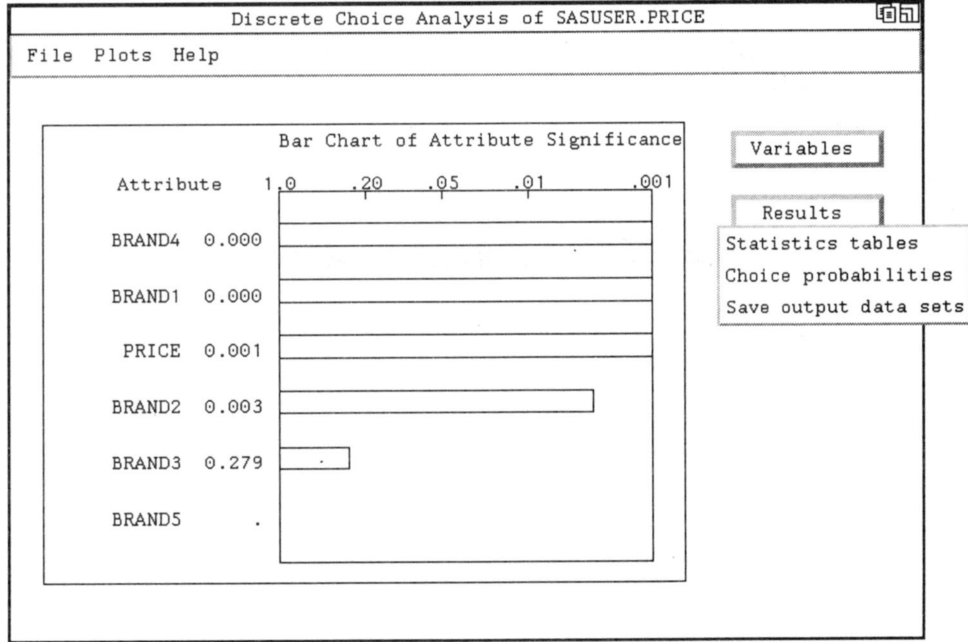

Figure 27. Bar Chart of Attribute Significance

You can view further analysis results by clicking the Results button. Select **Statistics tables** to view statistics on model fit as well as parameter estimates, and select **Choice probabilities** to view the choice probabilities for each choice set. You can save the choice probabilities, residuals, and parameter estimates by selecting **Save output data sets**.

Discrete Choice Analysis Probabilities

File Help

Choice Probabilities for Each Choice Set

SET	BRAND1	BRAND2	BRAND3	BRAND4	PRICE	Prob.
1	0	0	0	1	5.99	0.344
1	1	0	0	0	5.99	0.249
1	0	1	0	0	5.99	0.188
1	0	0	0	0	4.99	0.110
1	0	0	1	0	5.99	0.109
2	0	0	0	1	3.99	0.289
2	1	0	0	0	5.99	0.282
2	0	1	0	0	5.99	0.213
2	0	0	0	0	4.99	0.125
2	0	0	1	0	3.99	0.092
3	0	0	0	1	3.99	0.296
3	1	0	0	0	5.99	0.289
3	0	1	0	0	3.99	0.161
3	0	0	0	0	4.99	0.128
3	0	0	1	0	5.99	0.126
4	0	0	0	1	5.99	0.373

Figure 28. Choice Probabilities from Discrete Choice Analysis

If you select **Choice probabilities**, you see from Figure 28 that Brand 4 at a price of $5.99 is the most likely choice among the alternatives in choice set 1 (probability of 0.344). Brand 3 at a price of $5.99 is the least likely choice among the alternatives in choice set 1 (probability of 0.109). These choice probabilities help you see how your product performs against competitive products at various price levels.

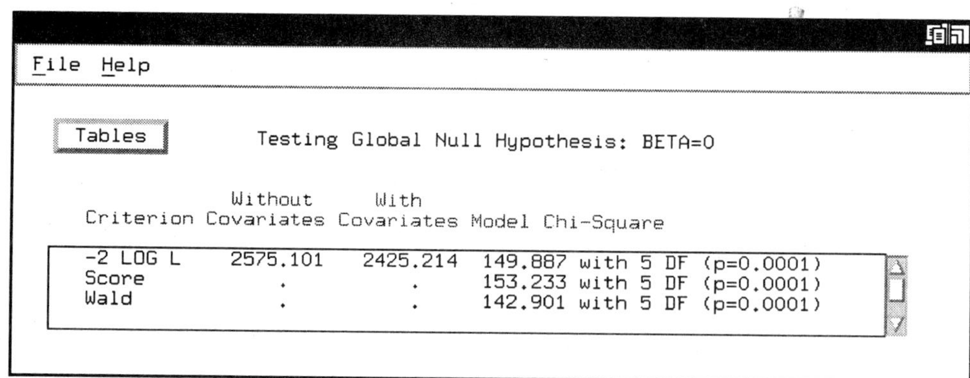
File Help

Tables

Testing Global Null Hypothesis: BETA=0

Criterion	Without Covariates	With Covariates	Model Chi-Square
-2 LOG L	2575.101	2425.214	149.887 with 5 DF (p=0.0001)
Score	.	.	153.233 with 5 DF (p=0.0001)
Wald	.	.	142.901 with 5 DF (p=0.0001)

Figure 29. Tests of the Global Null for Discrete Choice Analysis

Selecting **Statistics tables** displays Chi-square tests of the null hypothesis that all the parameter estimates are actually zero, which, in this case, you reject. (Note that in both the individual-level and aggregate analyses, the Chi-square statistics and *p*-values are the same.) These tests are shown in Figure 29.

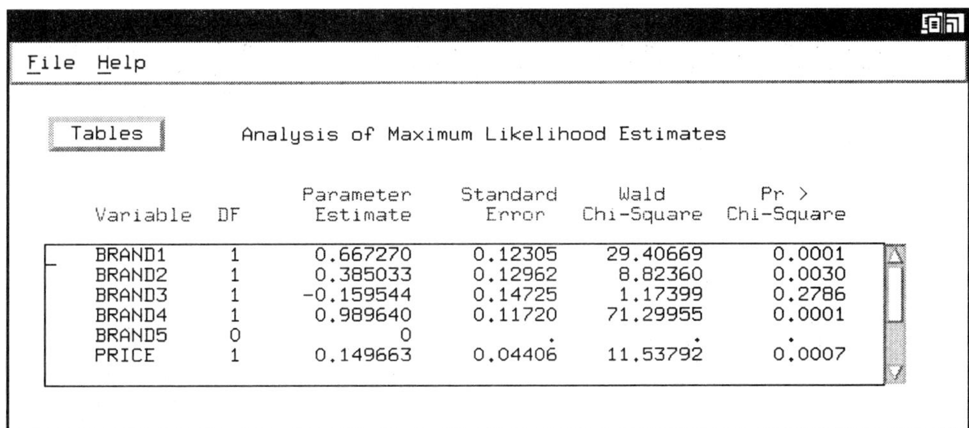
File Help

Tables

Analysis of Maximum Likelihood Estimates

Variable	DF	Parameter Estimate	Standard Error	Wald Chi-Square	Pr > Chi-Square
BRAND1	1	0.667270	0.12305	29.40669	0.0001
BRAND2	1	0.385033	0.12962	8.82360	0.0030
BRAND3	1	-0.159544	0.14725	1.17399	0.2786
BRAND4	1	0.989640	0.11720	71.29955	0.0001
BRAND5	0	0	.	.	.
PRICE	1	0.149663	0.04406	11.53792	0.0007

Figure 30. Parameter Estimates from Discrete Choice Analysis

Clicking the Tables button and selecting **Parameter estimates** displays Figure 30, which includes the parameter estimates, their standard errors, and a Wald chi-square test for testing that the parameter estimates are zero. The *p*-values are displayed in the bar chart in Figure 27.

Performing New Analyses

From the **File** menu in the discrete choice analysis window (Figure 27), select **Combine Data sets** to return to the Discrete Choice Data Representation window. In this window, you can specify one or two data sets and frequency variable or no frequency variable. If you make a mistake in specifying either of these options, you can correct it and redo the analysis.

Choose **Close** from the **File** menu in the Discrete Choice Analysis Probabilities window (Figure 28) to return to the discrete choice analysis window containing the initial plot (Figure 27). To redo the same analysis with the same data set but different variable roles, click the Variables button to return to the variable selection window. To start a new analysis, choose **New data set/analysis** from the **File** menu on the discrete choice analysis window.

References

Ben-Akiva, M. and Lerman, S. R. (1985), *Discrete Choice Analysis: Theory and Application to Travel Demand*, Cambridge, MA: The MIT Press.

Carson, R.T.; Louviere, J.J.; Anderson, D.A.; Arabie, P.; Bunch, D.; Hensher, D.A.; Johnson, R.M.; Kuhfeld, W.F.; Steinberg, D.; Swait, J.; Timmermans, H.; and Wiley, J.B. (1994), "Experimental Analysis of Choice," *Marketing Letters*, 5(4), 351–368.

Kuhfeld, W.F. and So, Ying (1994), TS273 Marketing Research Methods in the SAS System, Cary, NC: SAS Institute Inc.

Louviere, J.J. and Woodworth, G (1983), "Design and Analysis of Simulated Consumer Choice of Allocation Experiments: A Method Based on Aggregate Data," *Journal of Marketing Research*, 20 (November), 350–367.

Manski, C.F. and McFadden, D., eds. (1981), *Structural Analysis of Discrete Data with Econometric Applications*, Cambridge, MA: The MIT Press.

Multidimensional Scaling

Seven subjects rate their perceptions of similarities (on a 1 to 7 scale) between pairs of beverages, with 1 indicating very similar and 7 indicating very different. The beverages are milk, coffee, tea, soda, juice, bottled water, beer, and wine. There are 28 possible pairs of these eight beverages, and all subjects indicate their perceptions of similarity for each of the 28 possible pairs of beverages. The goal of the analysis is to determine which beverages are perceived by consumers as being similar.

Selecting the Input Data Set

The BEVERAGE data are *distance* data because larger responses indicate a greater perceived difference between two beverages. Alternatively, if larger responses indicate a greater perception of similarity, then the data are *similarity* data.

The BEVERAGE data has the following form (only the data from one subject are displayed).

Note: Only half the table for each subject is entered because the distances are symmetric (for each subject, the distance between milk and coffee is assumed to be the same as the distance between coffee and milk).

```
data beverage;
   input name $ milk coffee tea soda juice botwater beer
                wine beverage $;
   datalines;
Subj1  1 6 6 7 7 7 7 7  milk
Subj1  0 1 1 7 7 7 7 6  coffee
Subj1  0 0 1 7 5 4 7 5  tea
Subj1  0 0 0 1 5 3 5 4  soda
Subj1  0 0 0 0 1 5 3 2  juice
Subj1  0 0 0 0 0 1 6 6  botwater
Subj1  0 0 0 0 0 0 1 1  beer
Subj1  0 0 0 0 0 0 0 1  wine
...[48 other records]
;
```

On the Select a Data Set and Analysis window (shown in Figure 1 on page 7), select SASUSER from the Library list, select BEVERAGE as the data set, and select Multidimensional Scaling from the drop-down list of analysis possibilities. A message window informs you that multidimensional scaling requires either similarity or distance data; click the Continue button. To proceed with the analysis, click the OK button.

Defining the Variables

In the Multidimensional Scaling Variable Selection window (Figure 31), specify the variables MILK, COFFEE, TEA, SODA, JUICE, BOTWATER, BEER, and WINE as the objects by selecting them from the Variables list and clicking the Object button. It is crucial that the order of the objects is the same as their order in the rows of the data set. Also, specify BEVERAGE (the beverage names) as the ID variable and NAME (the subject identifiers) as the SUBJECT variable by selecting them and clicking the Id button and the Subject button, respectively. Because the data are ordinally scaled, the ordinal measurement level, which is the default, is appropriate for this example. The other measurement levels are interval, log interval, ratio, and absolute; you can select the appropriate level from the drop-down list to the right of Measurement Level.

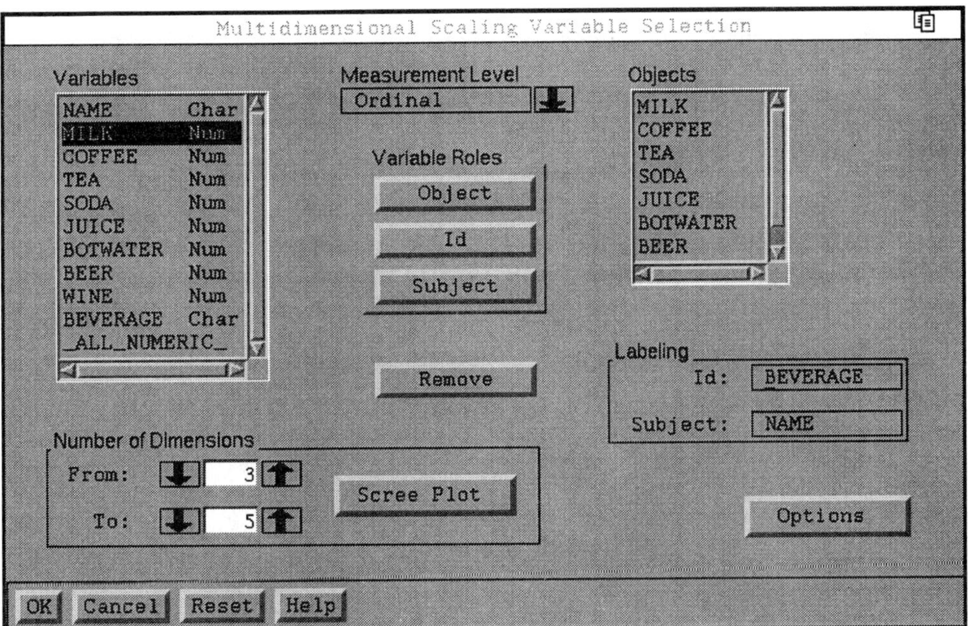

Figure 31. Multidimensional Scaling Variable Selection

From the Multidimensional Scaling Variable Selection window, you can access various analysis options that can be adjusted according to the type of data you are analyzing. For example, if you think that your subjects may use different perceptual schemes for judging similarity, you can choose to perform an individual differences analysis. Click the Options button to display the Options for Multidimentional Scaling Analysis window (Figure 32), and select Individual Differences Analysis. The data are distances (the default) because larger numbers represent more difference (less similarity). If the data are similarities, select Similarities in the Type of Data box. From the Fit Transformation box, you can select a transformation to be applied to both the data and the distances (or similarities).

- Fit Data to Distances applies no transformation.
- Fit Squared Data to Squared Distances squares all values before the model is fit; this gives more importance to large data and distances when fitting the model.
- Fit Log Data to Log Distance gives more importance to small data and distances when fitting the model.

You can select the method of standardization applied to the badness-of-fit criterion from the Fit Criterion Standardized by box.

The data for each subject comprise a matrix with the row and column entries corresponding to the subject's perception of the difference between the beverage of the row and the beverage of the column. If your data matrices are not symmetric, you can specify that the analysis be performed on the whole matrix by selecting Square from the Matrix Shape list box. Often, the matrix is symmetric, in which case you should select Triangular. Transformations that correspond to the measurement level selected are applied to each partition of the data individually. Select from the Data Partition list box to specify how you want the data partitioned. Click the Iterations button to specify the quantities: maximum number of iterations, gradient convergence criteria, and monotone convergence criteria. To close the Options window, click the OK button.

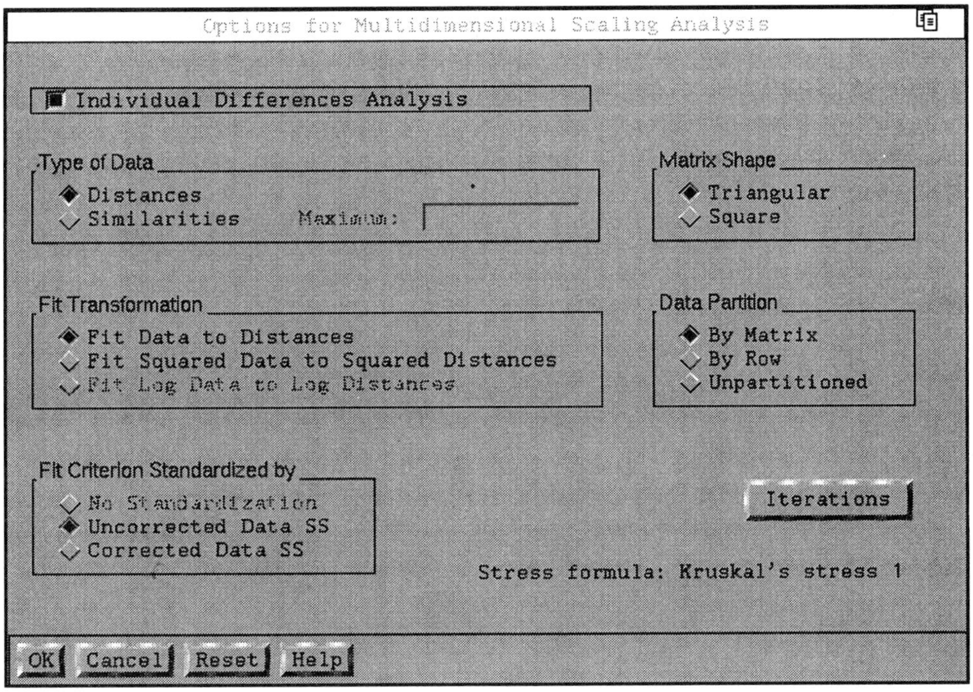

Figure 32. MDS Analysis Options

As in correspondence analysis and multidimensional preference analysis, you can set the number of dimensions for the solution. With multidimensional scaling, you can also solve for several multidimensional solutions in one analysis by setting the From and To numbers in the Number of Dimensions region of the variable selection window (Figure 31). Solutions are provided for all dimensions beginning with the number in the From box and ending with the number in the To box. In this example, choose three-, four-, and five-dimensional solutions either by entering 3 in the From box and 5 in the To box or by clicking the arrow buttons to set these values. A scree plot of the eigenvalues may be useful in determining the appropriate number of dimensions. You can create a scree plot by clicking the Scree Plot button.

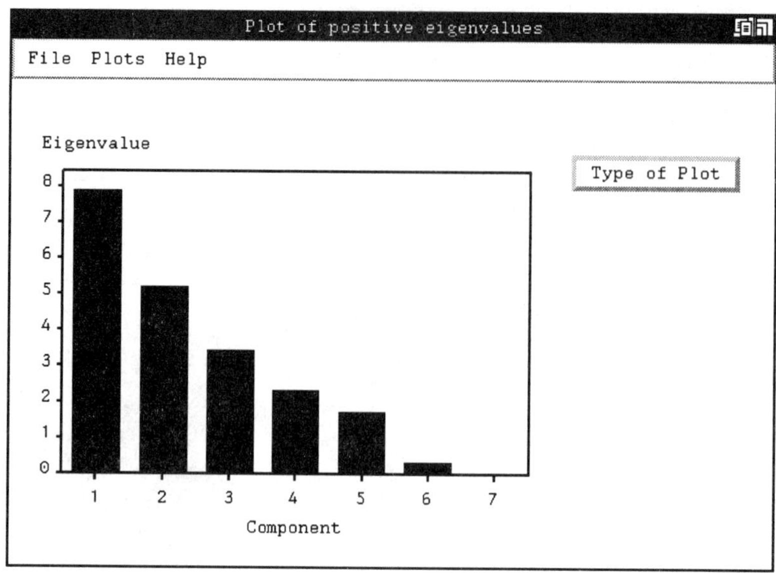

Figure 33. MDS Scree Plot

In a scree plot, look for the value on the horizontal axis where the magnitude of the eigenvalues plotted appears to drop and level off. In Figure 33, this occurs at component 6, which indicates that as many as five dimensions may be appropriate. When more than one analysis is requested, you can click the Type of Plot button to display a badness-of-fit criterion by dimension plot (stress plot). After closing the Scree Plot window, click the OK button to perform the analysis.

Accessing the Analysis Results

The analysis produces the multidimensional scaling window (Figure 34), which contains a coordinate plot of the first two dimensions of the three-dimensional analysis. If more than two dimensions are requested in the analysis, you can click the Plot button to display the Select Dimensions to Plot window (Figure 35) and specify which two dimensions are plotted. If more than one analysis is requested, you can use the Configuration: drop-down list to choose which multidimensional analysis is used for the plot. Also, when an individual differences analysis is performed, you can plot the coordinates of each dimension or the coefficients of each dimension. The Id variable is used to label the points of the coordinate plot, and the Subject variable is used to label the points of the coefficient plot.

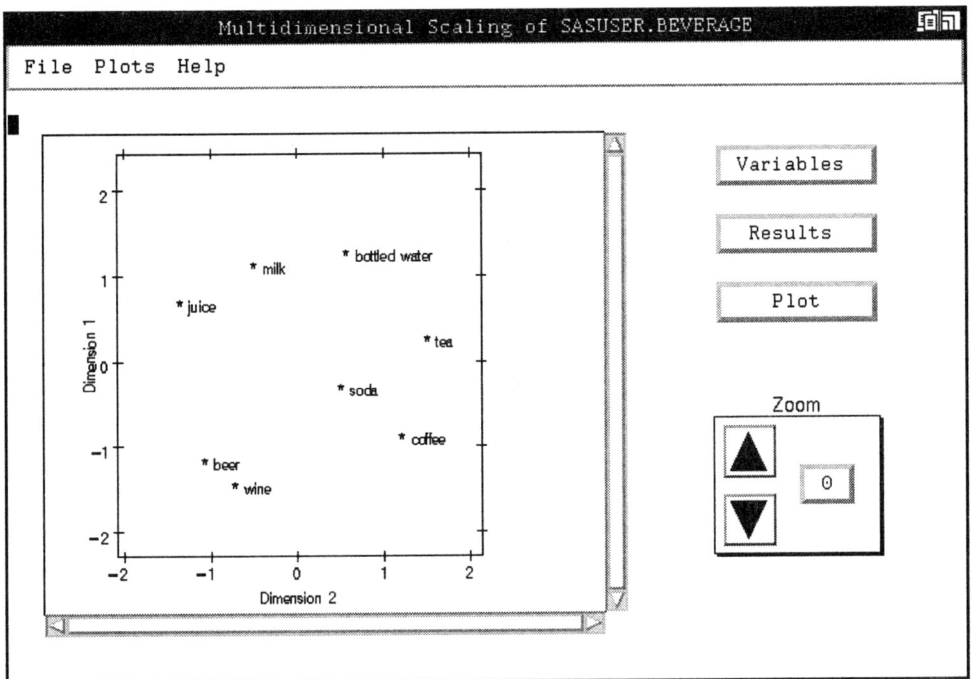

Figure 34. MDS Analysis Coordinate Plot

The plot interpretation has two aspects:

- finding a reasonable interpretation for each of the plot dimensions
- finding a reasonable interpretation of the relationship of the points

The presence of bottled water, milk, and juice at the top of the plot and wine, beer, and coffee at the bottom of the plot may indicate a sustenance versus recreation interpretation for the vertical dimension, Dimension 1. The interpretation of the horizontal dimension, Dimension 2, is not as apparent.

The plot shown in Figure 34 contains three clusters of points, signifying that consumers consider these products to be similar to each other: beer and wine; soda, tea, and coffee; and juice, milk, and bottled water. These relationships indicate which types of beverages compete with each other for market share.

You can obtain the coefficients plot for an individual differences analysis by clicking the Plot button and selecting Coefficients instead of Coordinates.

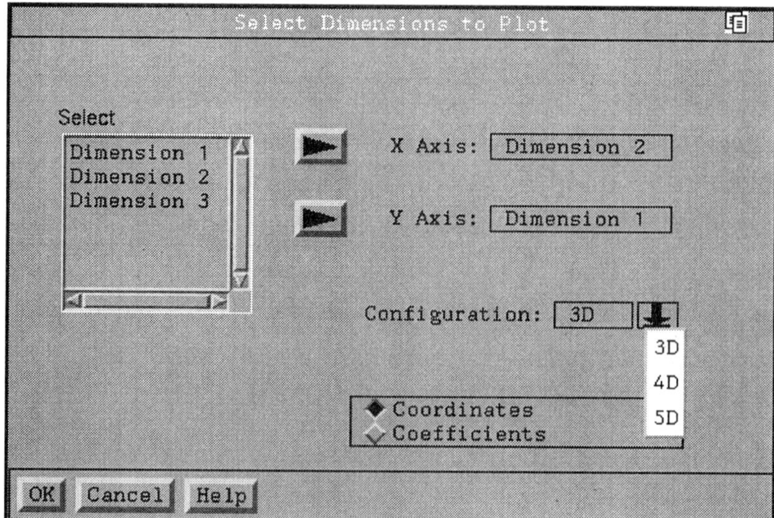

Figure 35. MDS Plot Options

In an individual differences analysis, there is a common perceptual map for all subjects, but different subjects have different weights for each dimension. In Figure 36, Subj4 is highest on the vertical axis and lowest on the horizontal axis. In other words, Subj4 weights whatever Dimension 1 represents more than the other subjects, and it weights whatever Dimension 2 represents less than the other subjects.

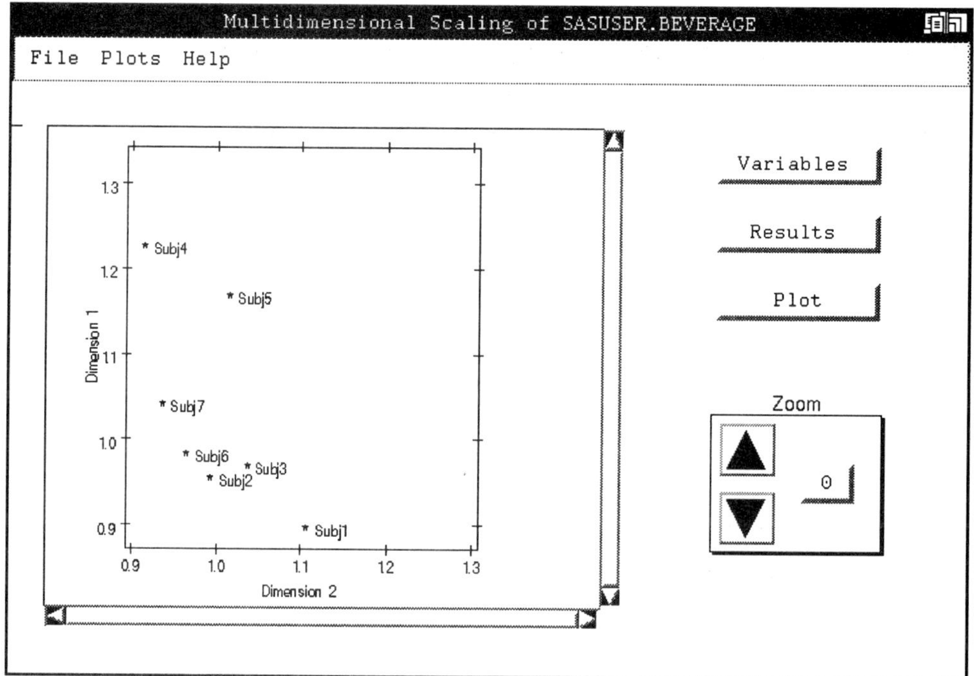

Figure 36. MDS Analysis Individual Coefficients Plot

It is possible that Subj1, Subj2, Subj3, Subj6, and Subj7 may cluster together and Subj4 and Subj5 may be outliers. Additional subjects may sharpen this possible clustering or eliminate it. Multidimensional scaling is useful in market research for discovering possible perceptual perspectives used by consumers and for revealing possible market segments.

You can view other analysis results by clicking the **Results** button.

Fit statistics	measures of how well the data fit the model: badness-of-fit criterion, distance correlation, fit correlation
Configuration table	coordinates (and coefficients) used in the plots
Residual plots	various plots used to assess the fit of the model graphically
Iteration history	information about the number of iterations and how the criterion changed over the iterations
Save output data sets	save coordinates, coefficients, residuals, and badness-of-fit statistics

Performing New Analyses

To redo the analysis with the same data set but different variable roles, click the **Variables** button to return to the variable selection window. To start a new analysis, select File from the menu bar on the multidimensional scaling window and then select New data set/analysis.

References

Davison, M.L. (1983), *Multidimensional Scaling*, New York: John Wiley & Sons, Inc.

Kruskal, J.B. and Wish, M. (1978), *Multidimensional Scaling*, Sage University Paper series on Quantitative Applications in the Social Sciences, 07-011, Beverly Hills, CA: Sage Publications.

Null, C.H. and Sarle, W.S. (1982), "Multidimensional Scaling by Least Squares," in *Proceedings of the Seventh Annual SAS Users Group International Conference*, Cary, NC: SAS Institute Inc.

SAS Institute, Inc. (1997), *SAS/STAT Software: Changes and Enhancements through Release 6.12*, Cary, NC: SAS Institute Inc, 1167.

SAS Institute Inc. (1996), *Marketing Research: Practical Applications Using the SAS System Course Notes*, Cary, NC: SAS Institute Inc.

Schiffman, S.S., Reynolds, M.L., and Young, F.W. (1981), *Introduction to Multidimensional Scaling*, Orlando, FL: Academic Press, Inc.

Torgerson, W.S. (1958), *Theory and Methods of Scaling*, New York: John Wiley & Sons, Inc.

Young, F.W. (1987), *Multidimensional Scaling: History, Theory, and Applications*, R.M. Hamer ed., Hillsdale, NJ: Lawrence Erlbaum Associates.

Multidimensional Preference Analysis

In this example, 25 consumers are asked to indicate their preference for 17 different cars. A preference scale of 0 to 9 is used, with 0 indicating very weak preference and 9 indicating very strong preference. The goal is to see where consumer preferences lie with respect to these 17 cars.

Note: This example is also described in the chapter for the PRINQUAL procedure in the latest version of the *SAS/STAT User's Guide*.

Selecting the Input Data Set

The CARPREF data set in the SASUSER library contains the data for this example. From the data set selection window (shown in Figure 1 on page 7), select the CARPREF data set, then select MDPREF analysis. Click the OK button to proceed. A message window appears to remind you of the required data layout for MDPREF analysis (Figure 37). For the CARPREF data, each row contains the consumer ratings for one model.

The data are created with the following DATA step:

```
data carpref;
   input make $ 1-10 model
              $ 12-22 @25 (judge1-judge25) (1.);
   datalines;
Cadillac   Eldorado     8007990491240508971093809
Chevrolet  Chevette     0051200423451043003515698
...[15 other records]
;
```

Click the Continue button to proceed to the MDPREF Analysis Variable Selection window.

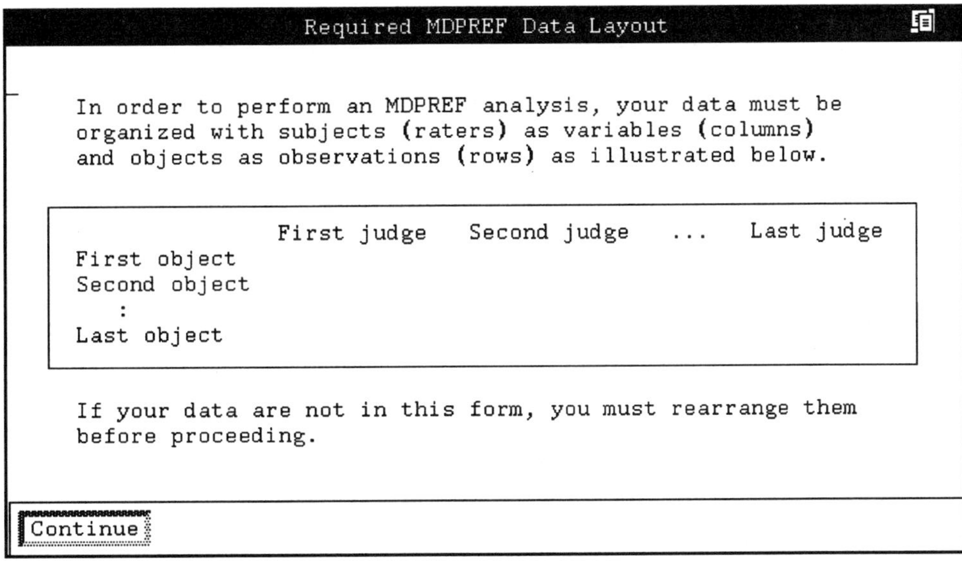

Figure 37. Required MDPREF Data Layout

Defining the Variables

As in conjoint analysis, you can choose to perform a metric or nonmetric analysis. In the Preferences region (Figure 38), click the down arrow button and select the desired measurement type from the drop-down list. Less frequently used types are available under the Other... selection. The measurement type is used for all subsequently selected Preference variables. Preference variables with different types can be used. For this example, use the Metric measurement type. Specify the respondents JUDGE1, JUDGE2, ..., JUDGE25 as Preference variables by selecting them in the Variables list and clicking the Preference button. Also, specify MODEL as the Id variable by selecting it in the Variables list and clicking the Id button. Clicking the Reset button clears all these choices.

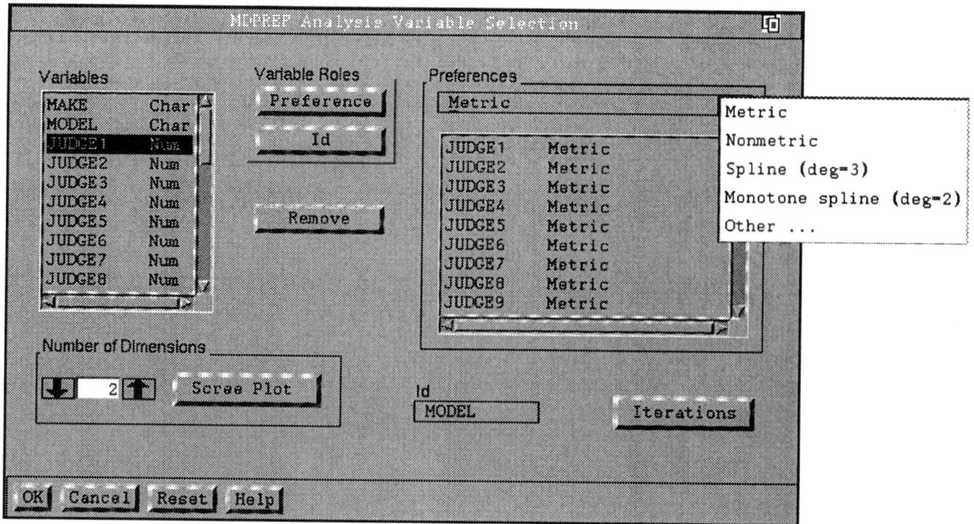

Figure 38. MDPREF Analysis Variable Selection

Click the Iterations button to set the maximum number of iterations, minimum criterion change, and minimum average change in standardized variable scores. You also can set the number of dimensions for the analysis; the default is 2. A scree plot of the eigenvalues is useful in determining an appropriate number of dimensions. To display the scree plot, click the Scree Plot button.

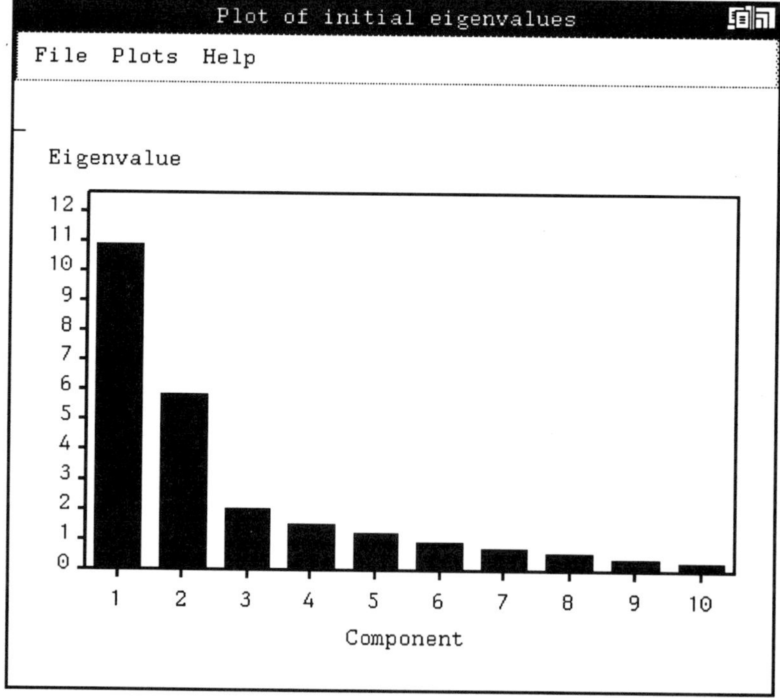

Figure 39. MDPREF Scree Plot

The plot (Figure 39) shows that the magnitude of the eigenvalues falls off for the first two dimensions, then levels off for the third and remaining dimensions. From this graph, you can determine that two dimensions appear to be appropriate. After closing the Scree Plot window, click the OK button to perform the analysis.

Accessing the Analysis Results

The plot on the multidimensional preference analysis window (shown in Figure 40) contains points for the 17 car models and vectors for the 25 respondents. The clustering of the car points leads to an interpretation of the dimensions. The vertical dimension separates Japanese and European from American cars in the upper half and lower half, respectively. The horizontal dimension separates small cars and large cars in the left and right halves, respectively.

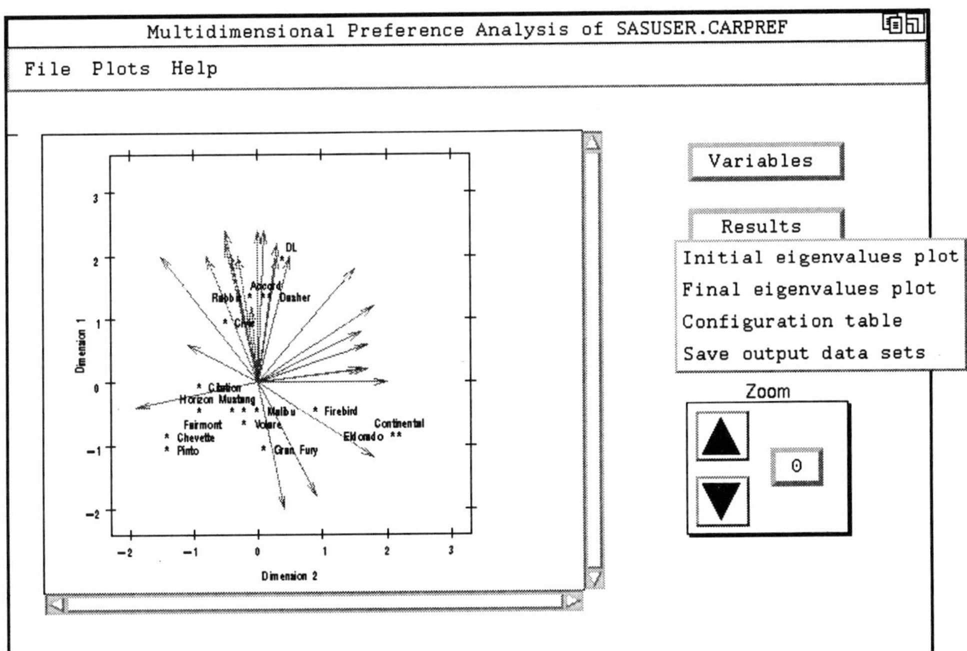

Figure 40. MDPREF Analysis Plot

Respondents prefer cars with points that are in the direction pointed to by their vector. Notice that many of the respondents prefer Japanese and European cars, while few prefer American cars. Also, there are a number of vectors in the upper right quadrant of the plot but there are no cars. This quadrant represents large, perhaps luxury, Japanese and European cars. This lack of available products to satisfy consumer preferences indicates a possible marketing area to pursue.

You can view other analysis results by clicking the Results button.

Initial eigenvalue plot	same as the scree plot shown in Figure 39
Final eigenvalue plot	another scree plot (which is the same as the initial eigenvalue plot when the Metric measurement type is used)
Configuration table	coordinates for the car points and the respondent vectors
Save output data sets	save coordinates used in the plot

Performing New Analyses

To redo the analysis with the same data set but different variable roles, click the Variables button to return to the variable selection window. To start a new analysis, select File from the menu bar on the multidimensional preference analysis window and then select New data set/analysis. To exit the Market Research Application, select End from the File menu.

References

Carroll, J.D. (1972), "Individual Differences and Multidimensional Scaling," in *Multidimensional Scaling: Theory and Applications in the Behavioral Sciences (Volume 1)*, R.N. Shepard, A.K. Romney, and S.B. Nerlove eds., New York: Seminar Press.

SAS Institute Inc. (1996), *Marketing Research: Practical Applications Using the SAS System Course Notes*, Cary, NC: SAS Institute Inc.

SAS Institute Inc. (1989), *SAS/STAT User's Guide, Version 6, Fourth Edition, Volume 2*, Cary, NC: SAS Institute Inc., 846.

Printing and Saving

Input Data Sets

From the Select a Data Set and Analysis window (shown in Figure 1 on page 7), you can view any data set by clicking the View Data button and selecting Data values from the pop-up menu. Select File from the menu bar of the data view window (Figure 41) to edit the data, save the changes, and print the data set.

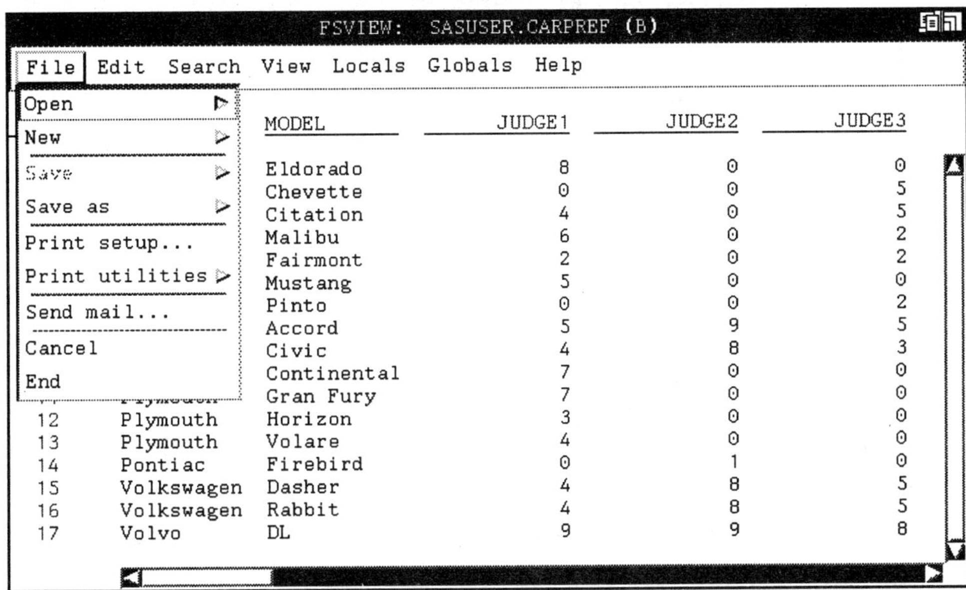

Figure 41. File Menu of Data View

You can also select the File menu (shown in Figure 10) on a main analysis window to view the data as well as to edit, save, and print the data set.

Note: These capabilities require SAS/FSP software.

Plots

Each window that contains a plot or graph has a **Plots** menu. From the **Plots** menu (Figure 42), you can change the colors used in the plot, print the plot, and specify the graphics device with which the plot is printed. You can print to plotters, printers, and cameras. You can also save the plots in various file formats, including GIF, JPEG, PostScript, and TIFF. Select **Change graphics device...** from the **Plots** menu, click the Device button and select **Export**. Then select the desired export device. Help is available for choosing an appropriate graphics device for output.

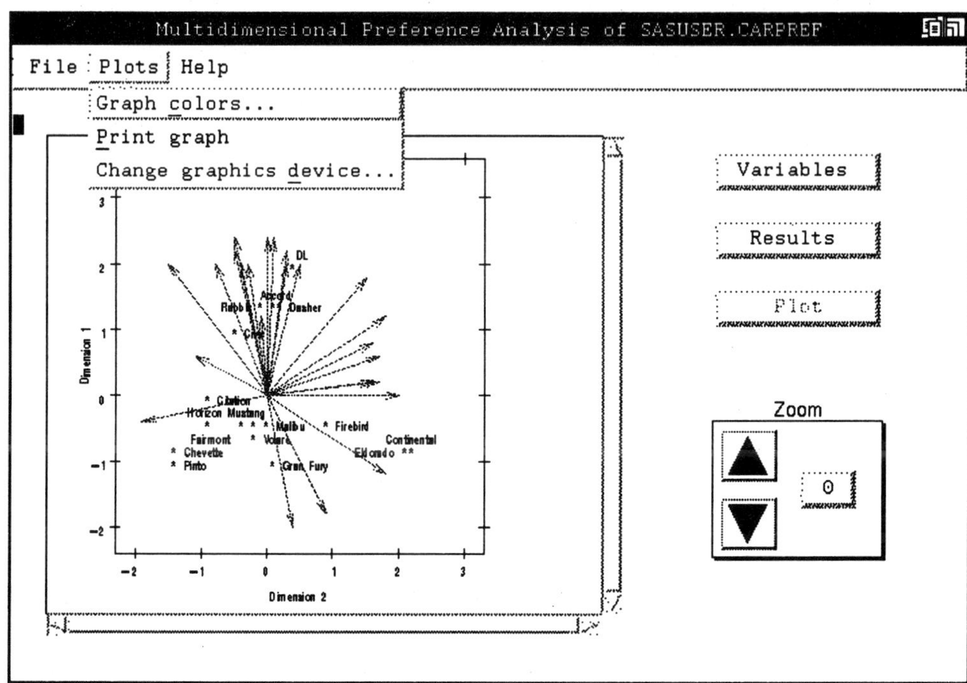

Figure 42. Plots Menu

Analysis Results

Each window that contains analysis results has a File menu. From the File menu (Figure 43), you can select Analysis summary to print and save a summary of the analysis that you perform, or you can select Text to print and save the contents of the current window. The Analysis summary indicates the variable roles used in the analysis. Analysis results are printed and saved as plain text (ASCII).

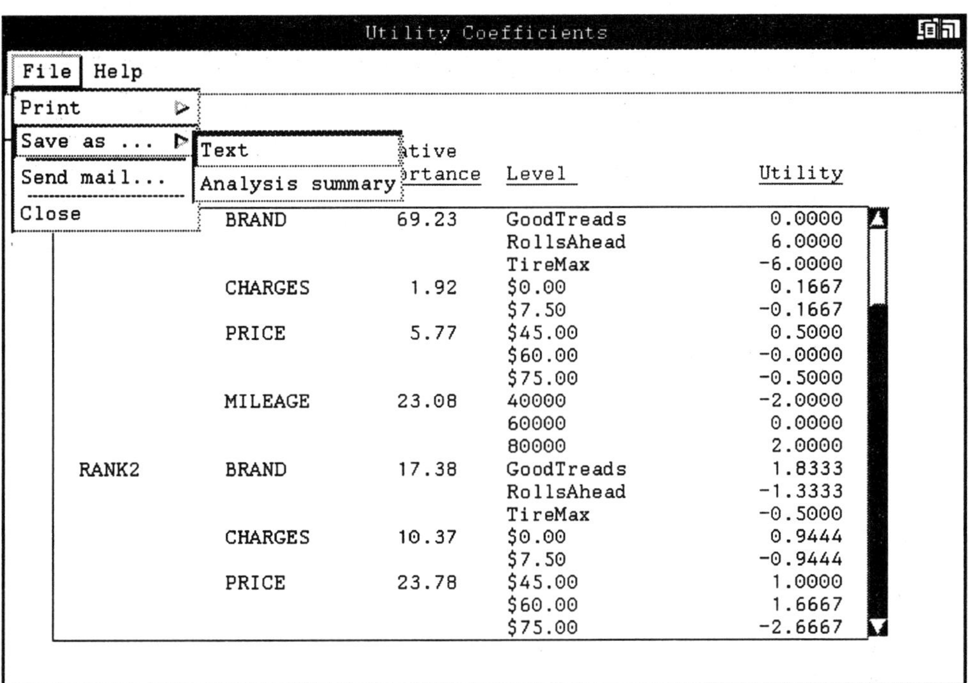

Figure 43. Saving Analysis Output

Output Data Sets

You can view, save, and print all data sets output by the SAS procedures that you use to generate the analysis you select. Click the Results button on any of the main analysis windows (for example, as shown in Figure 3 on page 11) and select Save output data sets from the pop-up menu. These data sets are saved as SAS data sets, and they can be used in further analyses.

Updating Samples for Release 6.12

This documentation reflects sample data set additions and revisions since Release 6.12. The changes are summarized in the following table:

Data Set	Analysis
TIRES	Conjoint Analysis
PRICE	Discrete Choice

After creating the sample data sets with the Market Research Application (see page 7), you should update the sample data sets. To obtain the correct materials, download the file **mra.dat** and submit it to the SAS System. This text file is available from the SAS Technical Support web page at

http://www.sas.com/techsup/download/stat/mra.dat

Alternatively, you can FTP the file by connecting to **ftp.sas.com** and using the command **get /techsup/download/stat/mra.dat** at the prompt. After you submit the file to the SAS System, your SASUSER directory contains the revised TIRES and PRICE data sets.